Neither Left nor Right

American University Studies

Series I
Germanic Languages and Literature

Vol. 59

PETER LANG
New York · Bern · Frankfurt am Main · Paris

Kurt Fickert

Neither Left nor Right

The Politics of Individualism
in Uwe Johnson's Work

PETER LANG
New York · Bern · Frankfurt am Main · Paris

Library of Congress Cataloging-in-Publication Data

Fickert, Kurt J.
  Neither left nor right.

  (American university studies. Series I, Germanic
languages and literature ; vol. 59)
  Bibliography: p.
  1. Johnson, Uwe, 1934-   —Political and social
views. 2. Individualism in literature. I. Title.
II. Series.
PT2670.036Z67 1987   833'.914   87-3698
ISBN 0-8204-0494-2
ISBN 0721-1392

CIP-Kurztitelaufnahme der Deutschen Bibliothek

Fickert, Kurt J.:
Neither left nor right : the politics of individu-
alism in Uwe Johnson's work / Kurt Fickert. --
New York; Bern; Frankfurt am Main; Paris:
Lang, 1987.
  (American University Studies: Ser. 1, Germanic
  Languages and Literature; Vol. 59)
  ISBN 0-8204-0494-2

NE: American University Studies / 01

© Peter Lang Publishing, Inc., New York 1987

Printed by Weihert-Druck GmbH, Darmstadt, West Germany

CONTENTS

CHAPTER 1

ART AND/OR POLITICS

Since nothing comes into being and continues to exist
in a vacuum, all art, the non-utilitarian product of creative activity, contains elements of the sociopolitical
climate in which it was created; even a hermetically sealed
poem by Georg Trakl or a Pollock canvas is tinged with the
spirit of its age.   Therefore, the much debated question
of whether or not a work of art may or should have political
implications only affords an occasion for a discussion
of the extent to which art participates in the process of
governance, the interaction between the individual and the
group.   The argument advanced by many artists, among them
George Orwell, an author who is also a social critic, that
art or specifically "writing is a thing apart"[1] represents
a wish rather than a point of view.

Literature, in particular, which cannot separate itself
from the sphere of words functioning simultaneously on the
non-aesthetic level of the passing on of information, is the
least suitable vehicle for conveying an esoteric experience.
Even in the magic world of the Grimm Märchen, as well as in
that of Alice in Wonderland, social status plays a con-
spicuous role, and economic considerations initiate the
bizarre chain of events of "Jack and the Beanstalk."   Not
only the words themselves but also the themes in a literary
work derive a part of their energy from their relationship

to sociopolitical tensions. In his study **The Literature of
Commitment**, Charles I. Glicksberg comments on the contention
that art exists in a private realm out of the reach of confrontations with society; "the writer's vaunted freedom to
write as he pleases," he avows, "is a pure fabricated myth:
the literature he actually produces springs inevitably out
of the clashes and collisions of contemporary values."[2]
However, the issue of the extent to which an artist or
writer may devote himself to an elucidation of societal conflicts remains, and will always remain, to be addressed.

The most radical attempt to restrict the intrusion of
the everyday world of social interaction, specifically a
bourgeois world, on the seclusion of the artist occurred in
the early nineteenth century while Romanticism reigned in
Germany. Then and subsequently, in all the Western world,
the cause of art for art's sake found its most fervent ad-
herents; retreat into the isolation of madness as the realization of this ideal is the possibility which haunts the
work of E.T.A. Hoffmann and Van Gogh. Describing the momen-
tum which the **l'art pour l'art** movement gained and maintained into modern times, the French critic Jean Gimpel has
summarized its sociological stance: "The romantic drew a
line of demarcation between his private and his public existence, between art, which was an integral part of his moral
life, and political life."[3] Gimpel cites the novelist
Gautier as a prime example of the romantic recluse, who dis-.

dained being identified with his country and its flag and vowed to disregard revolutions until bullets came crashing through the window (p. 98).

The twentieth century brought with it the inevitable reaction to this extreme form of the writer's alienation,[4] but the call for the writer to abandon his ivory tower soon became strident. He was asked not only to incorporate political factors in his work but also to become partisan. In an introductory essay to **Writers and Politics in Modern Britain, France and Germany,** John Flower indicates how, in the present, the writer's relationship to society has become central: "The political function of the writer is now seen as . . . the liberating of language itself from corruption and manipulation, not for the sake of aesthetic purity, but in the interests of social man."[5] The most trenchant instance of a writer's transition from a political position of advocating anarchy to one of complete commitment to a particular doctrine occurred in the career of Bertolt Brecht. In his work the egocentric anti-heroes of the early plays give way to protagonists who are at first victims of capitalistic exploitation and then altruists shaped by the dialectic process. The concepts of the **Lehrstück,** the teaching play promulgating a political creed, namely communism, and the epic theater, transforming the drama from a form of shared experience into an illustrated lecture on sociopolitical topics, were developed by Brecht into

methods for converting literature for the aesthetically inclined few into literature for the benighted many.

But subordinating the artist's individuality[6] to the
presentation of a consensus tended to produce propaganda
and not literature. Even playwrights who limited their
dramatizing to the piecing together of documentary material
could neither avoid bias nor ignore the restrictions imposed
upon them; their realism was but a blemished version of
historical truth. Hans Magnus Enzensberger, not only an
issue-oriented poet but also the author of a play dealing
sympathetically with the defense of the Cuban revolution,
has pointedly denigrated literature which espouses a political cause. In an essay entitled "Poetry and Politics,"
he establishes the dictum: "The political aspect of poetry
must be immanent in poetry itself and cannot be derived from
outside it."[7] In the same vein, contemporary critics have
reevaluated Brecht's work and concluded that its efficacy
lies not in its political persuasiveness but in its compelling portraits of beleaguered humanity. In his ap-
praisal of modern German literature, "The Dear Purchase,"
which deals with the price the artist pays for his individuality, J. P. Stern indicates the source of the strength of
Brecht's plays: "It is the affinity between corruptibility
and mercy in **Mutter Courage**, between exploitation and animal charm in **Puntila**, between sensuous delight, a high intelligence, cunning, and cowardice in **Galileo**--in fine, it

is the evocation of human freedom not beyond but inside history."[8] Stern saves his highest accolade for other authors like Hofmannsthal and Thomas Mann, who have insisted on maintaining their personal integrity even at the cost of having the relevancy of their work challenged; "their finest virtue," he writes, "is the paramount creative scrupulousness with which they anticipated, and sometimes attempted to oppose, those monstrous political solutions whose hallmark was cheapness and brutal simplicity, and which won the day" (p. 332).

The disastrous course of political events in Germany in the twentieth century acerbated the problematical nature of the writer's relationship to the society of his time. During the Wilhelmine era the conflict between authors who accepted the role of social critic--the naturalists--and those who espoused aestheticism--the neoromanticists--was debilitating in that neither camp was able to persevere. Although the expressionist movement which followed represented the amalgamation of political bias and esoteric writing, it was engulfed by the catastrophe of war and revolution. During the twenties there was a hiatus in the contention between an artist's impulse to commit himself to a cause and his need to stay apart. John Flower remarks that at the time of the first German republic the critical and artistic component of the nation was in tentative accord with the political: "In the Weimar period intellectuals on all sides enjoyed a rare rapport with their audience and a firm sense of their own 'representative' position, of their allegiance to a particular social group or class whose values and interests they were pledged to articulate."[9] Since, during the dozen years of dictatorship in Germany, significant writing was either suppressed or produced under the corrosive circumstances of exile, questions of the intermural relationship between art and politics did not arise. Subsequently, in the post-war era, they were of overwhelming importance. Authors who reestablished German literature as a literature of international import, such as Böll and Grass, acknowledged an obligation to deal with national guilt in the persecution of the Jews and the pursuit of war. After the economic miracle and the rise to prominence and stability of the **Bundesrepublik** these same writers took it upon themselves to stay critical in matters of governance; a few even participated in partisan politics. Concurrently, as exemplified by the founding of the **Gruppe 47**, a movement to reestablish the boundaries of the artist's social responsibilities manifested itself. Once again literature consisting of an impenetrable forest of esoteric symbolism won critical acclaim.

However, one aspect of Germany's post-war political situation was so cataclysmic in its effect on the German language itself and on German nationhood that it became incumbent on every author to contemplate it, at least in exploring his own identity as a German--the matter of the division of Germany into two countries, the matter of being either a West German or an East German. Confronting this dichotomy in German self-awareness, most writers have limited themselves to elucidating their relationship to one of the Germanies, the one in which their careers have flourished. Only one German author whose abilities are commensurate with his ambitions, Uwe Johnson, has undertaken the task of trying to fathom the affinities and disparities existing between the **Bundesrepublik** and the **Deutsche Demokratische Republik** and between their respective citizens. In four novels (one consists of four volumes) and a collection of shorter pieces, Johnson has endeavored, by depicting the involvement of the individual in the sociopolitical destiny of his country (both East and West Germany), to make a record through story-telling of the German experience in the waning years of the twentieth century. The subtlety of his conclusions on the impact of politics on the life of the individual gives his work universal significance. Mark Boulby has attested to its durability: "His [Johnson's] searching analysis of the connection between personal conflicts and universal moral problems, as worked out largely on an exactly defined plane of political existence, is an impressive contribution to world literature."[10]

In the face of the obvious thematic content of his

fiction, Johnson has not been reluctant to comment on his objectives. A novelist in a country where the poet is held in highest esteem and fiction has traditionally been hybrid in form--interspersed with poetry or interrupted by essayistic excursions, Johnson has emphasized his commitment to the prose narrative. "Was ich will," he has confided to Horst Bienek in a "workroom interview," "ist: eine Geschichte zu erzählen, mehrere Geschichten, die neu sind und interessant wegen ihrer Neuheit, wegen der in ihnen enthaltenen Erfahrungen und Kenntnisse, und zum anderen, weil das unterhaltsam genug ist."[11] The storyteller's task, he postulated on the same occasion, was to combine and at the same time keep separate the various strands that constitute the fabric of a character's life along with those in other characters' lives (p. 117). This process has as its goal, Johnson has suggested elsewhere, obtaining the absolute truth about the protagonist in the story, "die schwierige Suche nach der Wahrheit . . . Genauigkeit wird von ihm [dem Schriftsteller] verlangt."[12] Of particular importance in developing his stories, it can readily be discerned, is the attention the author must pay to the involvement of the individual in the social history of his time. "Accordingly," Johnson proposed on the television program "Literary Workshop," broadcast by the Bavarian schools television in 1973, "one might also call the novel a system of correlations, including the relation to social establishments or to the weather, to which each individual has, after all, his own, intrinsic relations."[13]   Because the course of history during his lifetime confronted Johnson with a variety of difficult political choices, allegiance to or defiance of a dictatorship, an occupying authority, a socialistic state behind prison walls, he developed a particular sensitivity to the intrusion of public circumstances on private morality.   The object of this study is to provide an analysis of his work in regard to Johnson's treatment of the theme of individual responsibility in achieving public good and simultaneously selfhood while maintaining one's integrity.   In reference to Hermann Hesse's politics, Samuel H. Hines, Jr., has called this problem "the essential dilemma of modern times" and has stated: "What is necessary is the simultaneous engagement of the individual in a process of self-examination leading to spiritual fulfillment ('know thyself') and in a process of presenting the self to others in a responsible way."[14]

One of Johnson's stories, included in the collection **Karsch, und andere Prosa**, "Jonas zum Beispiel," affords, as its title suggests, an archetypal example of Johnson's treatment of the theme of the individual confronted by political event.   The protagonist in this barely altered retelling of a biblical episode is Jonah, God's reluctant prophet.   He obviously symbolizes for Johnson the individual living contentedly out of the limelight who has a role in public life foisted on him. His first reaction to this intrusion on his privacy is flight. It is the paradigmatic solution arrived at by most of the characters in Johnson's fiction: Jakob in **Mutmaβungen über Jakob**, called upon to recruit for the East German espionage system, flees to the West and then back to an obscure destiny in the East. Karsch in Johnson's second novel reverses the order of Jakob's flight and in an appendage to the book, "Eine Reise wegwohin," tries to put both Germanies behind him in Italy. **Jahrestage** finds him still on the run in the United States. In **Zwei Ansichten** Fräulein D.'s escape across the border to the West is the story's central and basically only event. Finally, Gesine Cresspahl, a character in Johnson's fiction who has a great deal of autobiographical import, leaves the **Deutsche Demokratische Republik** with alacrity for a refuge in the **Bundesrepublik**, only to forsake it for an extended stay in the United States, where, however, she contemplates finding elsewhere a final haven, a "moral Switzerland." Her father has preceded her in resorting to flight by living in exile in England during the pre-Hitler era.

But Jonah's attempt to avoid commitment is thwarted. The boat on which he is escaping almost goes under in a storm, and he is cast overboard to appease the wrathful lord of the wind and waters. In Johnson's interpretation of the legend, the implication would seem to be that no man can choose to live a life outside of history, to turn his back

on the problematic existence of his fellow man. Through the
agency of the whale God saves Jonah for his mission. Para-
doxically, after Jonah has completed his task of diverting
the citizens of Nineveh from their wicked ways and thus
keeps them from being annihilated, he begins to feel that he
has been misused by a force which is capricious in nature,
alternately benevolent and sadistic. In answer to a question put to him by Wilhelm Johannes Schwarz, Johnson assigned a meaning to this story's course of events: "Es
handelt sich hier um einen Versuch, die Schwierigkeiten
zu erklären, in die ein Intellektueller kommt, wenn er sich
mit Macht affiliert und dann wegen taktischer Schwankungen
sitzengelassen wird."[15] This same denouement occurs frequently in Johnson's novels; in particular, it provides the
story of Fräulein D.'s escape from East Germany, her act of
political defiance in the face of the building of the wall,
with its ambiguous ending, since she does not become committed to life in the West, remaining rather like Jonah
under the castor bean tree in a personal limbo. Jakob's
faltering onto the path of an oncoming train is a similar
act of renunciation, a retreat from a common destiny into an
individual one. On this note of detachment from the idea of
letting oneself become the instrument of a political agency,
"Jonas zum Beispiel" comes to an uncertain end: "Und Jona
blieb sitzen im Angesicht der sündigen Stadt Ninive und
wartete auf ihren Untergang länger als vierzig mal vierzig

Tage? Und Jona ging aus dem Leben in den Tod, der ihm lieber war? [Is this a hidden reference to Jakob's fate?] Und Jona stand auf und führte ein Leben in Ninive? Wer weiß" (**Karsch, und andere Prosa**, p. 84); the stylistic device of ending two statements with a question mark and the ensuing question with a period is pertinent to Johnson's concept of the novelist's non-sovereign role.

Johnson's ability to retell an Old Testament story and to plumb its depths and give it contemporary significance indicates the resourcefulness which marks his work and provides it with its intensity. He is undoubtedly one of the major writers in post-war German literature; some critics[16] assign him together with Böll and Grass to a triumvirate of contemporary German authors who play a part in world literature. As an extraordinarily gifted writer he has had an unfortunately brief life span. He was born on July 20, 1934, in Cammin (also spelled Kammin), Pomerania in the northeastern costal regions of the German state--the day of his tenth birthday was one of the most ominous days in recent German history, the occasion of the foiled assassination of Hitler. As the family name makes clear, there were Swedish as well as German ancestors; both branches were farmers. Johnson's father was employed in the field of animal husbandry: he provided advice in an official capacity on matters of breeding and was also responsible for maintaining the quality of the milk on the market. As the war came to an end, he was taken away by the occupying Russian forces and interned in a labor camp in White Russia, where he died in 1947 or 1948; the exact circumstances of his death will never be known.

Together with a sister, Uwe Johnson grew up and attended school in the small town of Anklam. In 1944 he was selected to become a student at the "Deutsche Heimschule" in Posen, a boarding school for talented boys, established by the Nazi government. When, in 1945, the invading Russian troops came close, the students were dispersed, some pressed into service in defense of their country, others, Johnson among them because of his poor eyesight, permitted to take flight to the west. By his eleventh birthday he had begun an existence as a refugee at first in Recknitz in the district of Mecklenburg, then in Güstrow. The political ramifications of these events did not overwhelm him and compel him to become politically active, but rather reinforced his inclination to come to his own terms with the historic confrontations which were determining the course of his life. Although he had been admitted to a Nazi school, he was indifferent to the phenomenon of Adolf Hitler; "Nicht der Führer," he has since told an interviewer, "stand im Mittelpunkt meines Lebens, sondern meine Eltern."[17] Apparently, he did not hold a political system responsible for the death of his father while in Russian custody; it seems likely that he would have blamed the war. When he subsequently became a member of the East German youth organization, the **Freie Deutsche Jugend**, he only felt somewhat ill-at-ease: "Ich galt dort als bürgerlich," he contends. "Das ist nicht als Schimpfwort zu verstehen; es ist eine ideologische Bestimmung und bezieht sich nicht auf die Herkunft, sondern auf den persönlichen Standpunkt."[18] Already at an early age Johnson's propensity to find individual rather than political (common) solutions to contemporary problems manifested itself; he has himself described this lack of allegiance: "Zwischen den zehnten und sechzehnten Lebensjahr hatte ich auch keine politische Heimat, lediglich eine individuelle, persönliche Heimat."[19] Also evident was Johnson's interest in language and literature; his favorite subject in school, he has confided, was Latin. Without a doubt his living in Güstrow, where Ernst Barlach, one of the twentieth century's greatest sculptors and the author of a number of critically acclaimed plays, had made his home, influenced Johnson to choose a university education as the pathway to a literary career.

From 1953 to 1954 he studied Germanistik, the German language and literature, at the university in Rostock. In accord with German students' custom of changing universities for the sake of a professor or a course of lectures, Johnson moved from Rostock to the Karl Marx University in Leipzig, where he became a student of Hans Mayer, a prominent and much admired professor of Germanistik, who had

chosen after the war to serve the East German university
community. Difficulties arose as Johnson's studies at the
university were drawing to a close; he did not complete a
required examination because he felt that he had not made
sufficient progress in his work. Through the good graces of
Hans Mayer, Johnson was enabled to complete requirements at
a later date, but the episode in Leipzig had an aftermath.
Authorities in the East German educational system proved to
be less than enthusiastic about providing a post in his
field for Johnson, who now had the reptuation of a politically "difficult" student. Having returned in 1957 to
Güstrow, he worked on an occasional basis as a translator;
he is the author of the German version of John Knowles's
A Separate Peace and of Herman Melville's "Israel Potter."
With a co-translator he reworked the Middle High German
Nibelungenlied into modern German; to test their editor, the
two young men, whose contribution was being made anony-
mously, interjected occasional anachronisms in their revised
text, at least one of which escaped the editor's attention
and was printed. At the same time Johnson began writing his
first novel, **Ingrid Babendererde**; when the book was sub-
mitted to a publisher, it evoked interest but was rejected,
in part because of political implications in its contents
which the East German regime would find unsatisfactory. But
the publisher indicated that he would be eager to read Johnson's next work. With Johnson's assent, **Ingrid Babendererde**

was never published during his lifetime.

Indeed, Johnson was already busy with the story which would become **Mutmaßungen über Jakob.** The publication of this book by the West-German **Suhrkamp Verlag** in 1959 brought about his decision to leave East Germany for West Germany, a move which he has designated as an "Umzug," a change of residence, in actuality from East to West Berlin. Although he had not acquired the approval of the DDR authorities for his exit from their state (the immigration did have the sanction of the bureaucracy in the **Bundesrepublik**), he did not suffer the retribution of being denied access to East Germany until some time later. The occasion for Johnson's choosing to live in West Berlin had, after all, literary rather than strictly political overtones. Despite the fact that its protagonist was an East German worker, **Mutmaßungen über Jakob**, because of its ambiguities, could not have been published in the East. By a change of address, Johnson became a writer of repute **from** East Germany. About the same time Johnson's mother and sister moved out of the **Deutsche Demokratische Republik** to Karlsruhe in the West.

The critical success of **Mutmaßungen über Jakob** established Johnson in his career as an author. He was introduced to the members of the powerful literary society and tribunal, the **Gruppe 47**, and became the friend of Günter Grass. In 1960 he received the Fontane Prize for literary accomplishment from the city of West Berlin. In the next

year he spent four months in the United States as a guest of
Wayne State University in Detroit and of Harvard University
in Cambridge. Also in 1961 his second novel, **Das dritte
Buch über Achim**, was published. For nine months in 1962, as
the recipient of a governmental award, he had at his dis-
posal the facilities of the Villa Massimo in Italy for the
pursuit of his literary objectives. On this occasion he became involved in a journalistic controversy as the result of
a remark he made about the building of the Berlin wall at an
authors' conference. The literary critic and writer Hermann
Kesten took Johnson to task then and later in the press because he had not joined in the cry of outrage which the
erection of the Wall of Shame had elicited but had, instead,
proposed that for the East German authorities desperate
circumstances had necessarily called for desperate measures.
While the dispute over Johnson's loyalty to his adopted West
German homeland continued, he was awarded the Prix Inter-
nationale de la Litterature.

The collection of short pieces **Karsch, und andere Prosa**
appeared in 1964, and in 1965 the short novel **Zwei Ansichten**, the literary expression of Johnson's viewpoint in regard to the Berlin wall, was published. In the meantime,
Johnson had married Elisabeth Schmidt, whom he had met while
studying in Leipzig; together with her and their young
daughter Kathrina Johnson left Germany in 1966 for an extended stay in the United States. For two years he lived

with his family in an apartment in New York City, working
for a time for the publisher Harcourt, Brace and World on a
German language textbook--a collection of contemporary lit-
erature--and preparing all the while the material which
would constitute his next and last lengthy novel, **Jahrestage.** Subsequent to his return to Berlin, the first of the
four volumes of this epic appeared in 1970. The last volume
was published in 1983. A short narrative, **Skizze eines
Verunglückten,** and the text of a series of lectures on his
own work, **Begleitumstände,** had also appeared in the interim. During the night of February 23-24, 1984, Johnson died
in his residence on the Isle of Sheppey in England, where
he had been living in seculsion for some time, having ef-
fected a separation from his wife and daughter. The un-
expectedness of his death and the unexplicated circumstances surrounding it call for a consideration of the pertinence of the anomalistic premise that life copies art or
fiction, since Johnson's literary career and rise to prominence came about through his exposition of the sudden and
mysterious demise of his protagonist in **Mutmaβungen über
Jakob.**

FOOTNOTES

[1] Geoge Orwell, **Such, Such Were the Joys** (New York: Harcourt Brace, 1953), p. 71.   For an opposing view see Erich Heller, **Thomas Mann: The Ironic German** (New York: Paul P. Appel, 1973), p. 128:   "For a creative writer's politics cannot be detached, without loss of authenticity, from the nature of his imagination . . ."

[2] Charles I. Glicksberg, **The Literature of Commitment** (Lewisburg: Bucknell University Press, 1976), p. 58.   See also Karl H. Van D'Elden, "Introduction," **West German Poets on Society and Politics** (Detroit: Wayne State University Press, 1.979), p. 17:   "It is primarily the events of the times which, acting as a social or intellectual environment, consciously or unconsciously influence what a poet will write."

[3] Jean Gimpel, **The Cult of Art** (New York: Stein and Day, 1969), p. 95.

[4] See Glicksberg, p. 30, who emphasizes that the call for "commitment in the domain of the arts is a distinctly twentieth-century phenomenon."

[5] J. E. Flower, J. A. Morris, C. E. Williams, eds., **Writers and Politics in Modern Britain, France, and Germany** (New York & London: Holmes & Meier, 1977), p. 4.

[6] See Hans Mayer, **Outsiders: A Study in Life and**

Letters, trans. Denis M. Sweet (Cambridge, Mass.: The MIT Press, 1982), p. 5: "Literature is the province of the individual."

[7]Hans Magnus Enzensberger, **Critical Essays**, ed. Reinhold Grimm and Bruce Armstrong, trans. Michael Roloff (New York: Continuum, 1982), p. 27.

[8]J. P. Stern, "The Dear Purchase," **The German Quarterly**, 51:3 (May 1968), 329.

[9]John Flower, **Writers and Politics**, p. 3

[10]Mark Boulby, **Uwe Johnson** (New York: Ungar, 1974), p. 6.

[11]Horst Bienek, **Werkstattgespräche mit Schriftstellern** (München: DTV, 1965, **erweitert** 1976), p. 112.

[12]Uwe Johnson, **Berliner Sachen** (Frankfurt am Main: Suhrkamp, 1975), p. 21.

[13]Richard Sales, ed., **Motives**, trans. Egon Larsen (London: Oswald Wolff, 1975), p. 106.

[14]In Benjamin R. Barber & Michael J. Gargas, eds., **The Artist and Political Vision** (New Brunswick & London: Transaction Books, 1982), p. 154.

[15]Wilhelm Johannes Schwarz, **Der Erzähler Uwe Johnson** (Bern, München: Francke, 1970), p. 95.

[16]Cf. the obituary in **Newsweek** (March 26, 1984), p. 90,

which states: "With Günter Grass and Heinrich Böll [John-
son] is credited with creating a new German postwar literature."

[17]Schwarz, **Der Erzähler Uwe Johnson**, p. 95.

[18]Ibid., p. 96.

CHAPTER 2

MUTMASZUNGEN UEBER JAKOB: THE PERPLEXITY OF THE INDIVIDUAL
IN A CLOSED SOCIETY

Readers of **Mutmaβungen über Jakob** (**Speculations about Jakob**) can best approach the novel by imagining themselves to be members of a coroner's jury, assembled to determine the cause of a young man's death one foggy morning under the wheels of a train.   Like a coroner Johnson conducts the presentation of the evidence but scrupulously avoids organizing the testimony in a way that might influence the jury in reaching their conclusions.   The strangers paraded before them to testify about the circumstances leading up to the unwitnessed demise retain a great deal of their anonymity since they speak and even reveal their inner thoughts almost exclusively about their relationship to the deceased and leave their own lives unexplored.   Instead of a story leading to revelations Johnson provides ruminations, that is, speculations about his protagonist, who, of course, cannot himself have a part in the proceedings.   The outcome of the inquest, the answer to the question of whether Jakob's death was an accident, a suicide, or, remote as the possibility may be, a political assassination, is not to be found in the pages of Johnson's book, but rather in the minds of the jury, the readers.   So vague are the contours of the novel (in a sense the fog mentioned on the first pages never abates) that the publisher provided some editions of the work with a summary of the pertinent facts, essential for an intelligent reading of the text.

The unconventional stylistic features of **Mutmaβungen über Jakob** accounted for both the attention and critical acclaim it was accorded and the accomplishment of the goals which Johnson had set for himself in writing it. To present without prejudice his theme that one may not relinquish one's individuality for the sake of a [political] cause,[1] Johnson relinquished the role of omniscient author and created a mosaic of verbal pictures of Jakob, his protagonist, which, by exhibiting the personality as a juxtaposition of puzzle pieces, would duplicate life itself. The technique of providing the reader with a multilayered text, containing varied levels of perception of the author's story and theme, appears most prominently and successfully in the work of William Faulkner, and Johnson's encounter with Faulkner's **The Sound and the Fury** was, as Wilhelm Johannes Schwarz has pointed out, a decisive moment in his career.[2] For **Mutmaβungen über Jakob**, Johnson adopted and elaborated on Faulkner's stylistic device of telling the same story from different points of view; the most striking example of this technique in Faulkner occurs in **The Sound and the Fury** in a chapter relating the incoherent musings of a mentally retarded child. By presenting, instead of a narrative, the thoughts and conversations which a number of Jakob's friends and acquaintances have on the subject of the de-

ceased, Johnson has produced a novel which, he has contended, meets the most stringent requirements for versim-
ilitude set for contemporary fiction. "Der Verfasser sollte
zugeben," he has written, "daß er erfunden hat, was er vor-
bringt, er sollte nicht verschweigen, daß seine Inform-
ationen lückenhaft sind und ungenau . . . Dies eingestehen
kann er, indem er etwa die schwierige Suche nach der Wahrheit ausdrücklich vorführt, indem er seine Auffassung des
Geschehens mit der seiner Personen vergleicht und rela-
tiviert, indem er ausläßt, was er nicht wissen kann, indem
er nicht für reine Kunst ausgibt, was noch eine Art der
Wahrheitsfindung ist."[3]

What emerges from the dialogues between unnamed speak-
ers, the interior monologues of characters who reveal their
identities only to the perspicacious reader, and the narrative passages, sometimes vaguely, sometimes specifically
related to the novel's other sections, is both the outlines
of Jakob's personality and a glimpse into the people who are
speculating about him. The book's opening sentence, a
statement by the otherwise reluctantly present narrator:
"Aber Jakob ist immer quer über die Gleise gegangen" (p. 7),
is reaffirmed immediately by the first quotation, which
constitutes information supplied by Jöche, Jakob's co-
worker, a locomotive engineer (Jakob himself is a train
dispatcher); thereby the basic element in Jakob's character is firmly established. First the two remarks suggest

that the regularity which marks Jakob's way of going to work must also apply to his habits on the job: He is a conscientious worker. Secondly, the fact that he crosses the tracks diagonally allows the impression to arise that his steadfastness is such that it leaves room for the expression of individuality. The portrait of Jakob that Johnson creates brushstroke by subtle brushstroke, as the novel progresses or, rather, evolves, is that of a young man who combines to an admirable degree self-assurance with a keen sense of responsibility. Such is the admiration which Jakob's reliability evokes from his fellow workers and stewards in the workplace that, the reader is soon informed, "die Großen des Landes warfen ihr Auge auf Jakob" (p. 28); the biblical phraseology makes evident that this comment comes from Gesine, Jakob's adoptive sister and later love, whose speech sometimes reveals that she has an epic view of life. Since Jakob performs his demanding tasks so excellently in East Germany (possibly but not necessarily in Dresden) and the high quality of his achievement is recognized by the authorities, it must follow that he is as eager to be in a workers' state as it is eager to reward him for his allegiance.

The course of the novel charts Jakob's disenchantment with this supposedly ideal situation. The first breach in the wall of security Jakob has constructed around himself out of his faith in the good intentions of socialism and

the efficaciousness of the work ethic is made by the
flight of his mother to the West. Having been expelled
from their home by the Russian counter-invasion in 1945
and having lost husband and father in the war, mother and
son have found refuge in the coastal town of Jerichow in
the district of Mecklenburg. They have become guests in
the house of the cabinet-maker and widower Cresspahl, for
whose only child Gesine Mrs. Abs provides motherly attention. In the country which soon evolves into the **Deutsche Demokratische Republik** Mrs. Abs accommodates herself
to living in exile, while her son, having accepted the
validity of the description of the course of history presented to him by the socialist state and having been pre-
pared for and found employment in the state-run railroad
system, makes East Germany his home. In the meantime,
Gesine has grown up under the same difficult circumstances
but has rebelled against the indoctrination to which Jakob
has more readily succumbed. She leaves the Communist
satellite at a time when movement out of the East, especially by way of the four-zoned city of Berlin, is a matter of
enterprise and not of great danger. In West Germany she
becomes a secretary in the Nato complex in Düsseldorf.
Her position in the West makes her interesting to the
state security forces and espionage agency of the DDR.
Captain Rohlfs, a recruiter of spies for his government,
approaches Mrs. Abs with the request that she become an
intermediary in persuading Gesine to engage in counter-

intelligence operations. Mrs. Abs' reaction to this solici-
tation is unequivocal; "Nein," she says--it is the one word
by her quoted directly in the entire novel. At first, his
mother's flight is an anomaly to Jakob: she has traded a
life of honest work (she is a parttime cook in a hospital)
among friends for homelessness with bleak prospects in a
war-mongering society. Adding to his lack of comprehension
of her defection is the circumstance that she has been
unable to get in touch with him in order to explain the
reason for her sudden emigration.

In confronting Jakob with the reality of the choice
available to everyone to participate or not to participate
in the political machinations of a society, Johnson begins
his exposition of the conflict between the individual conscience and the state's policy of expediency. In the words
of Captain Rohlfs, the government's conscience constitutes
the principle on which it operates--the principle of necessity; the state does what it cannot avoid doing. At one
point, Rohlfs elaborates on this political philosophy:
"Was ist notwendig der Gruppe der 'guten, auch besten
Leute', damit sie gerechter Weise obsiege? Einigkeit
gegen den Gegner" (p. 122). But Jakob is not yet ready to
face the possibility that a dichotomy exists between the
will of the individual and the will of a group of good,
even the best people. When he is approached by the relent-
less Captain Rohlfs to use his influence on Gesine, he does

not panic but takes refuge in his job, the obligations of which he can fulfill without compromising his conscience.

But his mother's flight (Jakob is inclined to think of it as a change of residence) to the West has unsettled him to the extent that he recognizes that he needs to come to terms with it and must discuss it with Cresspahl, the man who has played a fatherly part in his life and who has, indeed, made the arrangements for his mother's departure from Jerichow. Jakob obtains a two-day leave of absence from his post in the dispatchers' tower and goes back to his adoptive home, arriving on Friday, October the seventeenth (the year is 1956).[5] There he meets another visitor to the Cresspahl household who contributes to his education in the field of the relationship between the individual and the political climate. The stranger to whom he is introduced is a tutor and assistant to the professor of English language and literature at the university in East Berlin and a long-time friend of Gesine, Dr. Jonas Blach. His reasons for seeking out Cresspahl's hospitality are never explicitly stated; he indicates, without further explanation, that he wants to be out of the limelight for a time. As a committed citizen of the East German socialist state, Blach is involved with others who are eager to work toward the suppression of Soviet hegemony in their country. They look to Hungary, whose revolution, they are aware, is about to occur, for an example of the quest for nonalignment, which

might also be pursued by the DDR. To mull over the pos-
sibilities which he sees on the horizon of the political
scene, Blach apparently needs the peace of a small town; in
addition, he has been informed by Gesine that "mein Vater
ist ein Turm" (p. 134)--a tower of strength. Providing
only speculations about Blach's motivation, Johnson nevertheless makes arrangements for an opportunity for Jakob and
Blach to confront one another, or for the politically committed intellectual to confront the politically committed
worker.

The topic with which these two similar and yet funda-
mentally dissimilar young men begin their discussion is
freedom. For Jakob this concept has no basis in reality
("Freiheit kommt nicht vor," p. 135); self-wareness exists,
however, from the very moment of birth. Blach counters that
he does not approve of substituting individuality for freedom, since the individual can separate himself from neither
the laws of physics nor the common lot of humanity. Having,
as he argues, the ability to affect the destiny of the
masses, Blach insists that he has an obligation to act
politically. Although Rohlfs must wait until the occasion
arises when he can participate in drawing such subtle dis-
tinctions, Johnson has previously allowed the viewpoint of
the Marxist to be expressed; his definition of freedom is
contained in the formula: "Freiheit die Einsicht in die
Notwendigkeit" (p. 123), by virtue of which individuality is

canceled out by the necessity that the state, as a totality, continue to exist. After Jakob's encounter with Blach has come to its inconclusive end, the dispatcher is left still clinging to the bastion of his confidence in himself and even associates this self-assurance with acceptance of the fact that his mother has left the state: "Und meine Mutter in die Flüchtlingsbaracken von Westberlin mit der Eisenbahn, und ich sorge dafür daβ sie alle sicher und pünktlich kommen wohin sie wollen" (p. 137). This ideal of self-sufficiency, freedom from social obligations except as they are fulfilled in the course of one's employment, is symbolized in **Mutmaβungen über Jakob** by Cresspahl's cat whose independence all the characters respect.

Equally free and unfathomable, Gesine Cresspahl makes an appearance at this point in the course of events. On Tuesday, the twenty-third of October, she arrives mysteriously in the city on the Elbe River where Jakob works. Johnson provides no accounting of and few speculations about her unexpected visit to the **Deutsche Demokratische Republik**. Equipped with a handgun and a miniature camera, she would seem to have set out to engage in espionage; however, she makes no attempt either to explain the presence of this equipment or to use it. Although no adequate clue to her motivation in undertaking her journey is given in **Mutmaβungen über Jakob**, Johnson's later novel **Jahrestage**, which delves at great length (to the extent of almost two

thousand pages) into Gesine's life, may afford material
for a well-founded supposition. In this story which takes
place some years after the foggy series of happenings in
Mutmaβungen über Jakob, Gesine has taken her and Jakob's
child to live in New York City. An employee of a bank with
dealings with the Czechoslovakian government about to break
free of Communist domination, Gesine plans to take advantage of a business trip to Prague to make a personal contribution to the country's fight for independence. This
kind of anti-authoritarian political activity may have
been foreshadowed in **Mutmaβungen über Jakob**, in which Gesine's return to East Germany on the eve of the Hungarian
revolution may have been prelude to an attempt to assist
Hungarian freedom-fighters. Whatever her intentions may be
in revisiting the other Germany, she is diverted from carrying out her plans.

Having waited for Jakob until his workday is over, Gesine puts herself in his charge. Making every effort to
remain unnoticed, they journey to Jerichow; they are, however, observed and followed by Captain Rohlfs of the secret
state police and his chauffeur-assistant. In what may be
called the climactic episode in the novel, if indeed the
attempt to obtain Gesine's services as an East German spy
is the pivotal point in the plot, all the principal characters are brought together under Cresspahl's roof--Gesine
and Jakob, Jonas Blach, Cresspahl, and the unexpected

arrivals, Rohlfs and his companion. A two-hour long conversation ensues, in which those assembled give voice to their reactions to the demand of the state that a citizen renounce self-interest for his country's sake. Jakob's mere presence represents, in fact, his contribution to the discussion, since his devotion to his job confirms his contention (never expressly put into words) that people are what they do, the circumstances under which they work notwithstanding. The faithful fulfillment of one's obligations in one's employment, Jakob is still sure at this point, is the hallmark of integrity.

Since, by adapting Faulkner's technique of supplying the reader with information only indirectly, Johnson has restricted himself to dealing with the events of his story retrospectively in conversations about them, the debate in the Cresspahl household occurs on the pages of **Mutmassungen über Jakob** only in bits and pieces of recollection. As is the case with Jakob's character, so the nature of the opinions expressed by Cresspahl, Gesine, Rohlfs, and Blach can only be speculated about (Jakob and Hänchen, the chauffeur-assistant to Rohlfs, participate as listeners). In the entire novel the intellectual Blach appears as a counterpart to Jakob the worker;[7] both are dedicated to the ideals of a socialist state, but Jakob's loyalty is unquestioning, whereas Jonas sees the government as an imperfect structure, presenting a constant challenge to those who are intent upon correcting its flaws. His visit to Cresspahl's house has come about ostensibly upon the recommendation of Gesine that he become acquainted with her father, a man of vast experience and great serenity, but actually for the sake of finding himself a secluded place, where he can prepare himself for the encounter between East German intellectuals and the Hungarian revolution--it begins on the morning after Gesine's arrival in Jerichow. The name Jonas itself contributes to a delineation of the character; related both to the biblical prophet Jonah and, by a stretch of the imagination, to the author Johnson,[8] it suggests recalcitrance, a disinclination to become the tool of those in power. For Johnson, as for Jonas, commitment to a cause, in both instances to socialism, does not supersede faith in the individual's sense of morality, where, indeed, commitment itself arises. Since political participation is the expression of a search for justice, a concept rooted in the personality, Jakob's contribution to the debate on the supremacy of the state over the individual is his conviction that in doing his job diligently he is fulfilling his obligation to a government which exists for the sake of the worker. Jonas envies him his self-assurance and tries at a later time in the novel to emulate him by studying him while he is at work in his tower. In the end, Jonas finds that he must remain true to himself and even allow himself to be arrested for activities which the socialist state considers to be counter to its interests; by means of these measures, however, Jonas feels he is doing his part to insure the system's efficaciousness. After Jakob's death, which in Jonas's view probably has been brought about by the undermining of his self-confidence through having reached negative conclusions about the political situation, the intellectual-activist is asked by Gesine why he does not choose to leave East Germany and elude imprisonment. "Ich habe etwas angefangen," he replies; "vielleicht will ich sehen was daraus wird. Dein Vater würde sagen: man kann nicht vor seinem eigenen Leben davonlaufen" (p. 216).

Selflessly devoted to service to the DDR, Rohlfs represents an opposing, but as Johnson proposes, equally viable position. Johnson has taken pains to make Rohlfs a sympathetic character. In acting on his political convictions, Rohlfs has martyred himself; when during the war he deserted and crossed over to the Communist lines, he was shot in the hand and leg by the German soldiers who witnessed his flight. These wounds could constitute the stigmata of the saint, since Christ's curcifixion resulted in injuries to his hands and legs (to hasten death the executioners sometimes broke the legs of those being crucified). In addition to his use of symbolism in making Rohlfs more than the unfeeling functionary, Johnson has allowed him to be generous, almost overly generous, in his

dealings with those with whom he must involve himself
in order to win Gesine over to the East German cause. He
does not put difficulties in Jakob's way because his mother
has fled the country. He is tolerant of Jonas and Cresspahl even though the former has associated himself with an
insurgent group and the latter has been known to embarrass
the regime by singing a song mocking it in public. He even
permits Gesine to return to West Germany at a time when
she has not yet committed herself to becoming a spy.

Therefore, when he expresses his convictions, they seem
personal rather than stereotypical, although they are
never in contradiction with Communist dogma. In the main he
argues that man as a social being needs to exist within an
entity and that communism is the only appropriate structure:
"Der Fortschritt eines Gemeinwesens ist abzulesen an dem
vernünftigen und gerechten Ausgleich der Einzelinteressen,
der Befriedigung der Egoismen" (p. 143). The goal of the
proletarian state, he contends, is reciprocity so that
each shall be working for the greater good of all: "daβ
einer den anderen am Leben hält" (p. 217). Accordingly,
Rohlfs finds spying to be the fulfillment of an obligation
and approaches Jakob, whom he considers to be as dedicated
to the cause of a socialist state as he is, without hesita-
tion when he needs assistance in persuading Gesine to use
her postion in the Nato organization to spy for his state
security system. However much fairness figures in Johnson's

characterization of Rohlfs, he does not hesitate to allow Rohlfs to make comments which would sound cynical to all but the already convinced. Thus Rohlfs quotes the Bible in order to justify Communist paranoia: "Wer nicht für uns ist ist gegen uns und ungerecht im Sinne des Fortschritts" (p. 186). Very much in the manner of Bertolt Brecht he explains further: "Es wird gefragt werden wer ist für uns und nicht wie gefällt dir die Nacht mit den dunklen Dörfern zwischen den Falten des Bodens unter dem mächtig bewölk- ten Himmel" (p. 186). The unshakability of his faith in the East German regime and the resultant expectation that all will eventually come to share his enthusiasm motivate him to call upon Jakob for his help in winning Gesine over and a bit later to allow both to visit Jerichow without authorization and eventually to leave it and the **Deutsche Demokratische Republik** for the West without hindrance.

Despite these blandishments on the part of Rohlfs and her love for her father and Jakob which ties her to the other Germany--perhaps even because of these factors-- Gesine decides, as the novel **Jahrestage** explains, to flee from the life she has established for herself in the **Bundes- republik** and distance herself, in the United States, from the events in **Mutmaßungen über Jakob**. This flight is an- other stage of the one undertaken by Gesine in her youth which was a sign of resistance to the forces of history, overwhelming individual destiny. In **Mutmaßungen über**

Jakob Johnson reports that Jonas has tried to delve into Gesine's motivation by asking a question which Jakob would scrupulously have avoided: "Warum bist du eigentlich dahingefahren?" Her answer is characteristically direct and yet equivocal: "Ich bin unglücklich gewesen Jonas" (p. 210). In **Jahrestage** Johnson apologizes to the reader for the ambiguity which sometimes obscures his description of the character Gesine; addressing the author, she informs him: "Meine Psychologie mache ich mir selber, Genosse Schriftsteller. Du mußt sie nehmen wie du sie kriegst."[10]

Gesine's personality contains elements of her father's dislike of ideologies and political cant and of her mother's need to give free reign to her responses to external pressures which threaten her inner security. Convinced as she is of the advantages of socialism, she nevertheless does not want it imposed on her. Here, her attitude resembles Jakob's, who, upon asking the question: "Soll einer sich selbst versäumen über einem Zweck," hears Rohlfs answer unabashedly: "Ja" and counters with the assertion: "Aber keiner, der nicht gefragt ist" (p. 156). Hansjürgen Popp has characterized Gesine's propensity to express her individuality on all occasions as "Andersmüssen."[11] She cannot live where there is no freedom of choice; she cannot be an advocate of communism or capitalism since the commitment to either kind of governance would deprive her of the ability to act in a personal way. The West German

government and its Nato allies cannot react to the advent
of the Hungarian Revolution except as political entities
and therefore are forced to stand helplessly by when the
Soviet military takes the country over. But as a single
human being Gesine can contribute to the fight for freedom.
The intervention of Jakob and her father, however, and the
meeting with Jonas and Rohlfs restrict her movements and
delay her in the execution of her plans. Perhaps through
these circumstances she recognizes the futility of the
course she has set out upon; perhaps her reunion with
Jakob and their falling in love provide her with an alternative course of action, the possibility of a family life
in the West, a substitute for a way of life in Jerichow
forever lost to her. When she leaves East Germany after a
two-day stay, she expects, it must be supposed, that Jakob
will soon follow her to the Rhineland. When he does and
then, because he finds that in giving up his position as
dispatcher he has given up his indentity, he returns to
the DDR, Gesine must acknowledge that her choice has been
nullified and she must pursue freedom and personal fulfillment in a different way. Even in **Jahrestage** her story
will have no pat denouement.

The life of Gesine's father, Heinrich Cresspahl, has
foreshadowed her own. He, too, became an exile at an early
age, both as a journeyman abroad and as a disillusioned
participant in the politics of the Weimar Republic, having

turned his back on the shabby manoeuvering of the socialists, whose cause he had espoused. Like Gesine after him
he falls in love during a brief visit back home; subsequently, he tries to keep his new bride with him in his adopted
country England. She is soon drawn back to Germany to meet
an untimely (or perhaps too timely) death like Jakob's,
although it is not as precipitous. The difference between
the lives of Gesine and Cresspahl lies in his having from
time to time been an active participant in the political
process; following the Second World War, he is appointed
mayor of Jerichow by the British occupying powers, and he
retains this post for a while when the Russians are given
control in the region. But as a consequence of what is
assumed to be anti-Russian behavior, he is put out of office
and imprisoned. Somehow he survives illness and a debasing
captivity and is able to rejoin his daughter. He remains
in Jerichow after her departure, even though his employment as a restorer of old furniture brings him little pro-
fit. To his own question of why he has stayed on in Jerichow, Jonas proposes an answer which the young and footloose
intellectual himself does not quite understand: "Weil er
ein Haus hatte" (p. 174 f.).

These events in Cresspahl's life have fashioned a
political philosophy , the basis of which is non-allegiance.
His contribution to the discussion in his home about individualism and commitment is his skepticism. "Das dumm'

Zeug mit den Menschenrechten" (p. 217) he calls the battle-
cry of the Western nations, since he believes that governments which necessarily act in their own self-interest
acknowledge only one right: the state has the right to be
right, as Rohlfs on another occasion has insisted. Previously, however, Cresspahl has also attacked the slogans
of the Eastern bloc; Johnson as a narrator in the book
reports: "Cresspahl hatte an der SACHE DES FORTSCHRITTS
wohl nichts mehr zu verteidigen gefunden (denn was war
das?), aber über dem UNBELEHRBAR ERGEBEN war er bedenklich
geworden" (p. 171; caps in the text). The phrase "intractably devoted" must represent to him the moral blindness of
those enslaved to a political cause. Having for a brief
time during the war undertaken to spy for the British, he
has in the immediate post-war era been the recipient of
their favor and of Russian disfavor; eventually the East
German communists will name a street in his honor for his
anti-Nazi activity, as the reader of **Jahrestage** becomes
aware. Because of his experiences, Cresspahl seeks by his
negativism to divert his daughter from her plans to take
up a political cause, be it spying for Nato or the DDR or
acting in behalf of the Hungarian freedom-fighters. Like
the biblical Jonah, who receives a call to become politically engaged and, having carried out the mission of a
capricious authority, spends the last years of his life in
disillusionment, Cresspahl is a wise old man who conspires

with Jakob and Jonas to make sure that Gesine will return quickly and safely to the West, where the freedom not to participate still exists at least as a possibility.

On Tuesday, October twenty-fifth, Gesine crosses the border back into West Germany with the assistance of Captain Rohlfs. Six days later Jakob finds another route out of the **Deutsche Demokratische Republik**, alone and on his way to Gesine. In pursuance of his intent to leave an explanation of Jakob's motivations up to the people who knew him best, who, however, can only provide speculations, Johnson makes the reasons for Jakob's westward trip as mysterious as the reasons for Gesine's eastward trip into the socialist state. In the interim before his departure, Jakob has presumably carried out his daily tasks. The only interruption in this routine existence has been the visit of Jonas Blach to the dispatchers' tower. Concerned about his own rebelliousness, Jonas has come there in order to discover the reason for Jakob's lack of it. A discussion ensues, the topic of which is the opportunity Jakob has had, together with his fellow-workers, to delay the transport of Russian troops and vehicles into Hungary. For his part, Jakob had decided that his job called for the smooth dispatching of all trains so that not only the Russian forces would be moved with alacrity but also his German countrymen on their way home from work. Jakob's response to the implied criticism that he might have helped the Hungarian revolutionaries

is that he could only have detained the Russians for an insignificant period of time. He calls acts of defiance such
as he might have participated in "Verrücktspielen." As if
to convince himself as much as Jonas and the others that his
decision was correct, he tells them: "Ich bin nicht trau-
rig" (p. 251). His friends note, however, that he hesitates
in leaving the tower at the end of his shift "als ob er
nicht wisse wohin nun gehen" (p. 251).

What the reader may infer from these implications is
that Jakob's self-assurance has been shaken; his departure
from the tower symbolizes the surrender of his belief in an
ideal, the conviction that commitment to a political cause
can occur without compromising one's integrity. Naturally,
the test to which the Russian attack on Hungary put him has
not in and of itself ruined the benign nature of his relationship as a worker to the workers' state. By way of
his mother's flight, Rohlfs' attempt to obtain his help
in recruiting Gesine as a spy, Gesine's reckless adventur-
ing, and the clashing views expressed in Cresspahl's kit-
chen, Jakob's confidence in himself and his way of life has
finally been undermined. Following the pattern Johnson has
established for several characters, that of flight from
commitment, Jakob leaves for the West, ostensibly not for
all time ("bleiben wollte er vom Anfang an nicht und nein,"
p. 280), but for the length of a visit with his mother and
with Gesine. He takes with him his doubts about the uses

of individualism and non-commitment: "Denn Cresspahl in der Ferne [Jerichow] und seine verschwundene Mutter und Gesines wahnwitziger Besuch, das alles half gar nichts, das waren wieder alles Leute mit ihren Handlungen **für sich allein** die einander nicht erklärten" (p. 525, my emphasis). For him Blach's definition of freedom as unrestricted exercise of one's conscience is still questionable: "Und daβ einer sich immer aussuchen kann was er will und verantworten **mag**: das nennst du Freiheit?" (p. 253, my emphasis). With these reservations in mind, Jakob cannot expect to begin a new life in the **Bundesrepublik** and to adopt its political philosophy. He stays only for a little over a week; it is time enough for him to be confronted with an instance of shabby political manoeuvering on the part of the Western powers--the Suez crisis; however, his reaction to Gesine's chagrin at this turn of events must be noncommital since she makes no mention of his response to it. The lure of a life of domesticity with Gesine likewise is quickly dissipated, since on Thursday, November the eighth, he leaves her, indicating his resolve not to return by means of a last-minute invitation to her--"Komm mit!" But the two lovers (for such they have become) like the two Germanies are, by dint of political circumstance, destined to go their separate ways.

The end of Jakob's story is the repetition of its beginnings: "Aber er ist doch immer über die Gleise gegangen"

(p. 300). The puzzlement over the manner of Jakob's death experienced by his friends and their author which led to Johnson's instituting an inquiry in the form of a novel remains unresolved for the reader. Johnson himself may not have intended to provide an answer to the riddle of how Jakob happened to be run down by a train, the scheduling of which he knew well.[12] Johnson offers no clear evidence that the supposition of an accidental death should be disallowed. In his book which establishes whatever facts underlie the novel's many ambiguities, Hansjürgen Popp provides what would be the only reasonable outcome of an inquest: "Man wird sich das Unglück als durch Unachtsamkeit verschuldet zu denken haben . . ."[13] The overtones of suicide or assassination which this misadventure on a foggy morning conveys are not meant, however, to be disregarded. Jakob's confusion caused by the undermining of his commitment to a political creed he considers to be just is without a doubt a contributing factor to his becoming the victim of an accident. Also pertinent is Rohlf's exhibition of lack of conscience in using Jakob's death as the occasion for persuading Gesine to meet again with him in West Berlin only three days after the fatality; this unrelenting devotion to his duty as a captain in the secret service could have a sinister aspect, if Rohlfs can be assumed to have determined that Jakob was returning in order to betray his country. But an eventuality of this kind, coupled with the supposition that Rohlfs would have planned and executed a political murder that would appear to be an accident, would necessarily be hyperbolic and counter to the novel's realistic, non-melodramatic tone.[14] The fact that the possibility of death by assassination exists is, nevertheless, a part of the book's thematic structure. Had Rohlfs become convinced that Jakob had defected and then had come back to spy for the West, he would as a loyal servant of the state have had no compunction about having him executed--he would, indeed, have been obliged to proceed in this way. It is Johnson's thesis that Jakob, who, caught between an oncoming and a departing train (one from the West, one from the East), jumps from the path of one into the path of the other and dies, is the victim of an inner conflict between the need for commitment and the loss of it. He has been a prime example of the right man in the right place--a worker whose devotion to his job is so complete that he has no other life outside of his tower, and who is a citizen of a country, the government of which exists for the sake of nuturing such dedication. The naturalness of Jakob's behavior which causes him to be admired for his singlemindedness rather than to be ridiculed for it has a similarity to the physical grace with which some people are born and which, as Heinrich von Kleist has pointed out in his essay "Ueber das Marionettentheater," they lose the moment when they begin to reflect on their capability. In a sense, **Mut-**

maßungen über Jakob is a book about the self-destruction of a hero; even more it is a satire on the propaganda novel which depicts the worker's progress through doubt and confusion to a commitment to the socialist state, to a recognition of his identification with that state. Instead of triumphing in this way, Jakob is caught in the middle between a private ethic and a sociopolitical one, between a personality and an occupation, and is crushed between the the two opposing forces.

For Johnson, individuality precludes commitment to political ends, no matter how just and appropriate they may be. In his essay on Johnson, "Registrator Johnson," Marcel Reich-Ranicki points to this bias in his work: "Johnson bekennt sich in seiner epischen Praxis zur programmatischen Unparteilichkeit."[16] In more than one instance, Johnson has himself disavowed allegiance to any political party or system; "persönliche Erfahrungen," he writes at one time, "hinderten mich immer, einer Ideologie rückhaltlos mitzudenken, mitzuerleben."[16] On this predeliction he has based Jakob's defeat which comes about because Jakob cannot live in a land where commitment is not required and cannot live with himself in a land where it is. Johnson has given further testimony pertaining to the downfall of the committed individual. Called upon to speculate about the fate of Jonas who has been imprisoned as a participant in a conspiracy against the state, Johnson speculates: "Jonas Blach

wurde 1964 entlassen aus dem Zuchthaus Bautzen und lehrt
seitdem Englische Literaturgeschichte mit einem krankhaften
Betonen der marxistischen Interpretationen von Sozial-
geschichte . . . Und das ist jemand, der nicht in die
Bundesrepublik gehen möchte . . . Und so wird keine west-
deutsche Reise oder westeuropäische Reise ihm die Augen
öffnen."[17] The novel's political message is that, although
the individual cannot avoid involvement in social history,
even by contriving time and again to flee from one country
and system to the next, he dare not consider surrendering
his critical faculty, his sense of right and wrong, and the
appreciation of his selfhood in order to achieve sociopolitical goals. When Jakob begins to question the wis-
dom of his decision not to delay the passage of the Russian troop and equipment trains to Hungary, he begins to
realize that he has in actuality sacrificed his integrity
and acted for expediency's sake. Inevitably, so Johnson
seems to suggest, political decisions are made to maintain
the authority of those in power. In explaining the meaning
of his short story "Jonas, zum Beispiel," he makes the same
point and adds the observation, equally pertinent in reference to the events in **Mutmaβungen über Jakob**, that those
who lend themselves to becoming the promulgators of political creeds are doomed to disappointment and abandonment.

The importance and durability of **Mutmaβungen über
Jakob** as a work of contemporary German literature are based

upon its relevance to the political and individual fate of Germans in a divided Germany, but Johnson has succeeded almost in spite of the book's ambiguities (among them passages written in dialect) in depicting the immersion of everyone who lives in the twentieth century in socio-political crosscurrents. And yet he has not written a political tract.[18] Instead, the novel serves the purpose of confronting readers with the necessity of maintaining their political and personal independence. Johnson's didacticism, a persevering tendency in German letters most recently reinforced by Bertolt Brecht, has been most aptly characterized by Mark Boulby: "Johnson aims in his writing not so much at any communication of feeling or, for that matter, an aesthetic effect, as at the unmasking of truth and stimulation of insight."[19] This exposition of the danger implicit in the imposition on the individual of an external system of values continued in Johnson's second, but actually third (counting the unpublished **Ingrid Babendererde**) book, **Das dritte Buch über Achim**.[20]

FOOTNOTES

[1]See the crucial question put by Jakob (whose words are sparse throughout the book): "Soll einer sich selbst versäumen über einen Zweck" [without a question mark], Uwe Johnson, **Mutmaßungen über Jakob** (Frankfurt am Main: Suhrkamp, 1969), p. 156. Further page references to the novel will be given in the text.

[2]Schwarz, **Der Erzähler Uwe Johnson**, p. 11: "Doch war es besonders **The Sound and the Fury**, das einen großen Einfluß auf ihn machte."

[3]Uwe Johnson, **Berliner Sachen** (Frankfurt am Main: Suhrkamp, 1975), p. 20.

[4]Although I do not think it necessary for the reader of **Mutmaßungen über Jakob** to be aware in every instance whose viewpoint Johnson is conveying, a completely reliable key to each situation has been supplied by Hansjürgen Popp in his book **Einführung in Uwe Johnsons Roman Mutmaßungen über Jakob** (Stuttgart: Ernst Klett Verlag, 1967).

[5]Eberhard Fahlke in **Die Wirklichkeit der Mutmaßungen** (Frankfurt am Main: Peter Lang, 1982) provides a conveniently condensed time scheme for the events in the novel.

[6]See Hansjürgen Popp, "Einführung in 'Mutmaßungen über

Jakob'" in **Ueber Uwe Johnson**, Reinhard Baumgart, ed. (Frankfurt am Main: Suhrkamp, 1970), p. 57: "Auf Katzen wenigstens wirkt sich die Veränderung, die durch den Sozialismus in die Welt gekommen ist, nicht aus . . ."

[7]See Kurt J. Fickert, "Biblical Symbolism in **Mutmaßungen über Jakob**," The German Quarterly, 54:1 (Jan. 1981), 59-63.

[8]See Schwarz, **Der Erzähler Uwe Johnson**, p. 20.

[9]Cresspahl has warned Gesine: "Jerchow kann di nich helpn" (p. 212).

[10]Uwe Johnson, **Jahrestage 4** (Frankfurt am Main: Suhrkamp, 1983), p. 1428.

[11]Popp, "Einführung in 'Mutmaßungen über Jakob'" in **Ueber Uwe Johnson**, p. 50.

[12]Cf. Schwarz, **Der Erzähler Uwe Johnson**, p. 28: "Der Leser kann es [wie Jakob stirbt] nicht wissen, denn der Erzähler Johnson weiß es selber nicht . . ."

[13]Ibid., p. 53.

[14]Once again **Jahrestage** affords insight into the problem. Political murder is explicated by way of a warning Jakob had received: "Du könntest zerquetscht werden zwischen zwei Waggons, oder von einem Zug stürzen, und keiner wüßte, was da passiert ist (**Jahrestage 4**, p. 1810).

[15]Marcel Reich-Ranicki, **Deutsche Literatur in West und**

Ost (Reinbek bei Hamburg: Rowohlt, 1970), p. 161.

[16]Schwarz, **Der Erzähler Uwe Johnson**, p. 93.

[17]Quoted by Fahlke, **Die** Wirklichkeit **der Mutmaßungen**, p. 237.

[18]See Robert Detweiler, "Speculations about Jakob: The Truth of Ambiguity," **Monatshefte**, 58:1 (1966), 25.

[19]Boulby, **Uwe Johnson**, p. 9. In a recent article on the relationship between the writer and politics, "Elfenbeinturm und Barrikade" (also used as the book's title), Johnson's con- temporary and an even better-known author, Siegfried Lenz, has commented both on the writer's inherent didacticism and his or her individuality. "Ich glaube," he proclaims, "daß Literatur von einer unwillkürlichen didaktischen Energie ge- tragen wird" (**Elfenbeinturm und Barrikade**, München: DTV, 1986, p. 13). With particular pertinence to Johnson's work (without referring to it directly), Lenz has also made this assessment: "Wo der Literatur an ihrer Integrität gelegen ist, da bleibt der Schriftsteller eine Ein-Mann-Partei" (p. 22).

[20]In **Begleitumstände** Johnson disclaims responsibility for the title, proposing that it was the least offensive of several choices given to him; see Uwe Johnson, **Begleit- umstände** (Frankfurt am Main: Suhrkamp, 1980), p. 175.

CHAPTER 3

DAS DRITTE BUCH UEBER ACHIM: THE USES OF COMMITMENT

Achim, the racing cyclist, whose biography the protagonist in **Das dritte Buch über Achim** undertakes to write, is almost a resurrected Jakob, one who has put his self-doubt and rebelliousness behind him in order to be able to give his complete allegiance to the East German state. The book's thin plot deals with the confrontation between Achim and his counterpart, the West German journalist and would-be biographer Karsch,[1] who swears fealty to no ruler or principality and becomes interested in discovering why someone would: "Und Achims Zusammenhang mit seinem Land (das Land und Achim selbst) war ihm unverständlich, das sollte er aufschreiben."[2] He fails in his endeavor to write the third book about Achim (two biographies already exist), and Johnson's account, again told retrospectively, attempts to analyze the relationship between two men and between a society in which the individual is permitted to disassociate himself from the politics of the state and one in which the individual is required to merge his identity with that of the state (cf.: "Achims Leben gehörte ihm nicht;" p. 195). Karsch's inability to complete his book about Achim symbolizes the incapacity of the West German citizenry to come to terms with the political stance of their fellow Germans who live across the border; thereby the possibility of the reunification of Germany, it is suggested, no longer exists. At the same time, particularly in a short story, "Eine Reise wegwohin," written in 1960 and published in **Karsch, und andere Prosa**,[3] which constitutes both a recapitulation of the events in **Das dritte Buch über Achim** and its epilogue, Johnson makes clear, since here Karsch leaves the **Bundesrepublik**, that conditions in West Germany are as lamentable as those in the East. The evenhandedness with which Johnson deals with the diverse halves of Germany has brought him the reputation of being "der Dichter des geteilten Deutschland"; he has renounced the title, however, on the grounds that he had never chosen the subject of the division as his topic: "Dieses Thema kriege ich täglich zum Frühstück, ohne daß ich die Zeitung lesen müßte," he maintained on one occasion.[4] Nevertheless, a note of explanation appears on the final page of **Das dritte Buch über Achim** which describes the book's purpose as the attempt to explore the quandry of a nation rent asunder; Johnson states in the addendum: "Die Ereignisse beziehen sich nicht auf ähnliche sondern auf die Grenze: den Unterschied: die Entfernung und den Versuch sie zu beschreiben" (p. 337).

This goal affects the style and determines the course of the novel. Instead of a convoluted arrangement of dialogues, narrative fragments, and stream-of-consciousness segments, **Das dritte Buch über Achim** has a reportorial format: there are questions put to the author, and his responses become a rather straightforward account of Karsch's three-month stay in East Germany. Johnson has indicated that the inquiries come over the telephone from Karsch's friends and coworkers in Hamburg who are curious about his adventures in the other Germany and has proposed that this narrative device enables the reader to share with the writer the experience of developing a story.[5] Despite the objectivity of this approach, the narrator's point of view is closely allied with that of Karsch, to the extent that Wilhelm Johannes Schwarz has taken them to be generally analogous: "Von allen Gestalten Johnsons ist wohl der Journalist Karsch seinem Schöpfer am nächsten verwandt . . ."[6] This intimation that some of Johnson's characters represent offshoots of his own personality has been supported by Johnson himself, who both in his works and his comments on them depicts himself (by name sometimes) and his protagonist as undergoing the same experience. In "Eine Reise wegwohin" Johnson carries his identification with Karsch even further by indicating that, after the events in **Das dritte Buch über Achim**, both retreat to Italy to begin a kind of life in exile. In the novel itself, it would seem, Karsch is more a point of view than a person, and an autobiographical (in an anecdotal sense) interpretation of the character would as a consequence have little pertinence. It is Karsch's function to stand for the West German mentality when it is confronted by an East German in the course of his daily life and in the throes of his commitment to the socialist state. All the people in the book serve as models,[7] and the plot consists of the presentation of a system of values, which the reader is called upon to pass judgment on.

Since the characterization is sketchy, motivation plays an insignificant role in the novel. Hans Mayer has put the matter of the characters' vague outlines succinctly: "Auf Johnsons Menschen ist nämlich kein Verlaß."[8] Therefore, the reader is ill-informed about the incident with which **Das dritte Buch über Achim** begins: Karsch receives a telephone call from an East German actress with whom he was once intimately acquainted, inviting him to visit her, and he decides that he would like to undertake a trip to another country. The book does not seek to answer the question of why Karin is interested in seeing an old friend from across the border. Johnson does not entertain the idea that she might want to discuss leaving East Germany. Since Karsch's dissatisfaction with some aspects of life in the West becomes clear only during and after his sojourn in the socialist state, his ready acceptance of Karin's invitation is likewise never accounted for. If Karsch means to renew a relationship, his intentions are abruptly thwarted, for he discovers at once that Karin is living with East Germany's star athlete and foremost celebrity, the

country's greatest racing cyclist, Achim. Upon meeting
him, Karsch becomes intrigued with the amiable young man's
poise, self-assurance, and sense of dedication. These
traits contrast with his own self-doubts and the lack of a
fixed purpose in life. To explore the differences between
them or to provide some diversion for himself during the
time when Karin cannot be with him--she is busy with her
activities as an actress--Karsch sets about gathering material so that he can write about Achim. Eventually the
East German authorities become aware that a somewhat prominent West German journalist is interested in pursuing the
subject of one of the country's finest athletes; the occasion seems to present itself for affording West Germans
some insight into the quality of the life led by those who
are dedicated to upholding the aims of the socialist state.
Accordingly, although Johnson does not deal directly with
their motivation, East German officials come to visit Karsch
and propose that he undertake to write for them yet another
book about Achim, in addition to the two which already
exist.

Critics have been quick to relate this fictitous
situation to the fact that the popular and highly respected
East German racing cyclist Gustav Adolf Schur, known af-
fectionately as "unser Täve," had indeed been portrayed
in two biographies--one an original and an updated version
by Klaus Ullrich. In regard to some incidental matters

Ullrich's text and Johnson's novel appear to overlap. Confronted with these analogies, Johnson took pains to make clear that they were the results of coincidence, asserting that he had not based his story on events in Schur's life, about which he knew little. In **Begleitumstände** he seeks to establish the authenticity of his characterization of Achim by placing portions of the Täve biography and his novel side by side in order to point out the differences. He fails to achieve the desired effect. To better purposes, he reveals that he had not begun with the idea that Achim would be a cyclist; rather, he would be a swimmer. This controversy about Achim's true identity need not be resolved; however, it serves to reinforce an analysis of **Das dritte Buch über Achim** based on the assumption that Johnson is intent upon writing fiction which is true to life in that it deals with questions of identity usually glossed over in conventional, "factual" biographies. In a newspaper article Johnson once posed clearly his concept of the effect which literature is supposed to achieve: "Sie [die Aufklärung, d.i., der Zweck des Erzählens] fordert von einem Leser dieser Erzählung nicht, daß er sich sofort verändert [cf. Brecht], sondern daß er die Geschichte aufnimmt, sie überdenkt und daraus seine eigenen Schlüsse zieht."[9] The Achim, that is, Gustav Adolf Schur, in Ullrich's biography is not meant to be the object of the reader's scrutiny; his story is told in order to reassure the reader that his adulation for the cyclist and admiration for a hero of the state are appropriate. On the other hand, the Achim of **Das dritte Buch über Achim** is a person who has lost his individuality and become in the main a symbol of dedication and commitment. Upon making this discovery, Karsch realizes that he as someone who feels he must be free to choose among alternatives cannot successfully write a book about someone who believes that there are none.

Previously Karsch has approached his work on Achim's biography with the assumption that he must set about documenting the development of the individual. He questions Achim about his early years--his relationship with his parents (Karsch eventually visits Achim's father), his misadventures as a youngster during the war and the occupation, his first bicycle, and his first experience of adolescent love. This research is intended to establish that Achim had had a part in determining the course his life was to take, that sociopolitical events had not simply swept him along. Karsch learns, for example, that a photo exists depicting a scene during the June 17, 1953, uprising against the East German regime in Berlin on which someone resembling Achim appears as someone in the crowd. For Karsch, the possibility that the exemplary Achim may have participated in an anti-government demonstration, or at the very least may have been interested in witnessing it, indicates that Achim is capable of expressing his individu-

ality, of wanting to use his own judgment. Another incident which Karsch uncovers in his exploration of Achim's
past revolves around a trip Achim probably made to West
Berlin to purchase a part for his bicycle unavailable in
the East; the question Karch would want to pose in his
book is whether or not the athlete would engage in an il-
legal transaction (according to the laws of the **Deutsche
Demokratische Republik**) in order to be able to perform
better in competition. For Achim, the question is irrelevant; the philosophy that the end justifies the means
which underlies the politics of communism (and fascism as
well) disallows moralizing, the exercise of conscience,
on the part of those who adhere to the principles of
absolutism.

The cooperation between Achim and Karsch in working on
Achim's biography becomes a confrontation between two men
whose private destinies have been shaped differently by
public events. Life in the socialist state has produced a
German compatriot whom a German from the West can hardly
understand. Even the language in the DDR, as Johnson
carefully points out, seems to be another kind of German.[10]
Therefore, Karsch decides that his mission to demonstrate
to the West Germans that East Germans are only separated
from them by "the border--the difference--the distance"
and not by a system of values must be abandoned; he will
not write the third book about Achim. It is, of course,

crucial to note that Johnson did. The author of **Mut-maßungen über Jakob**, which questions but does not disavow an East German point of view, has in his second published work also placed equal emphasis on the propensity of the countries in the West to allow their citizens to express their individuality. In this regard, Karsch and Johnson, too, now a resident of West Berlin, are critical of Achim's willingness to obliterate the personal past which is a part of his identity. In "Eine Reise wegwohin," the brief sequel to and an explication of **Das dritte Buch über Achim**, Johnson places Karsch more pointedly in a West German environment and identifies some of its negative aspects. Upon his return to the West from the DDR Karsch finds that no one is particularly interested in a conciliatory approach to East German intransigence; he becomes himself the victim of the prejudices of West German security forces who, suspecting that he might be a spy for or a terrorist from the East, conduct a search of his apartment for incriminating evidence. As a result of this and other exhibitions of the West German government's aggressive stance, Karsch flees to Italy. In summary, the critic Durzak characterizes Karsch as an individual disaffected by the politics in both parts of Germany: "Er verkör-pert den Intellektuellen, der sich mit der offiziellen westdeutschen Politik nicht zu identifiziern vermag, der auch gesellschaftlich in einem Zwischenbereich lebt."[11]

Karsch, in effect, foreshadows the Gesine of **Jahrestage,** the character with whom Johnson is, as he has indicated, most personally involved, who learns to practice the politics of individualism, searching for a country where the exercise of conscience is the one established sociopolitical principle. The narrator in **Das dritte Buch über Achim** proposes: "Westdeutschland ist nicht gerecht, Ostdeutschland ist nicht gerecht: vielleicht werden wir es eher" (p. 302).

The third and only other character of consequence in **Das dritte Buch über Achim** (the remaining ones are similar to the types found in expressionistic plays, e.g., a landlady) is Karin, Achim's present and Karsch's former lover. As is Johnson's custom, he associates the manner in which she makes her living with her **Weltanschauung,** her personal philosophy. Like Achim she is a performer, an actress, but while he expresses himself by perfecting a physical skill, she like Karsch has to deal with words. Both she and Karsch reflect on the situation in which they find themselves and act on the conclusions they draw on the basis of their experiences, rather than follow the custom of Achim, who makes the best of conditions imposed on him by accepting them without reservation. However, Karin has chosen to remain in East Germany, while Karsch pursues a restless course of flight from eastern Germany to the West in the aftermath of the war and then from the **Bundesrepublik**

to Italy. (In **Jahrestage** he has travelled even further, to
the United States, his life having been endangered by the
Mafia in Italy.) It has been suggested that Karin's choice
of remaining in the DDR might duplicate the decision of
the German actor Gustav Kieling who, having at one time
fled to the West, returned very quickly to the East to
stay.[12] But Karin more closely resembles Achim in this
regard, except for the fact that her loyalty to the East
German regime is a sham, a part of the role she has given
herself to play. She is a successful actress in both
her professional and personal life. Almost as popular
as Achim, she has reaped the rewards of becoming a symbol
for achievement in the socialist state without having had
to sacrifice her capacity to resist coercion. Her ability
as a player to maintain her identity while wearing a mask,
seeming to be someone else, serves as an example of the
type of resistance, perhaps the only type, possible for
those who have by dint of circumstance and the fortunes of
war been sequestered in East Germany. In the section of
Der deutsche Roman und die Wohlstandsgesellschaft dealing
with Johnson's novels, the authors have described Johnson's view of contemporary society, both in the East and in
the West, as an instrumentality for exerting pressure on
the individual to conform: "[Johnson] sieht den Menschen
als unter dem Druck historischer, örtlicher Umstände
stehend, unter dem der vorherrschenden Ideologien, unter

Zwang sich anzupassen oder wenigstens die Pose der An-
passung vorzuspiegeln, um eine Basis für die gesellschaft-
liche Existenz zu gewinnen."[13] Achim has become a victim
of sociopolitical oppression; Karsch escapes it by fleeing.
Karin fares better than both; she has outwitted the East
German authorities. Perhaps her invitation to Karsch to
visit her stems from a desire on her part to inform her
fellow Germans in the **Bundesrepublik** that the East Germans
are not to be written off, that most of them have resisted
and continue to resist becoming subservient to the practi-
tioners of power politics. Even her relationship with
Achim may be the expression of an effort to prevent his
succumbing to the blandishments of the Ulbricht regime.
Even though she fails in accomplishing this aim, she has
reason to believe that the East Germans who share her dis-
affection with the state probably have the hope that Achim
is dissembling as much as they are. Johnson has himself
proposed in a lecture given at Wayne State University in
Detroit that Karsch eventually comes to this conclusion:
"Er gelangt zu der Erkenntnis, daß die Achtung des Volkes
für Achim als Idealbild seiner selbst nicht ganz das sein
könnte wofür es in offiziellen Kreisen gehalten wird,
sondern daß die Achtung Achims vielmehr im Zusammenhang
mit dem Gefühl stehen könnte, er repräsentierte den einfachen Mann 'gegen die Regierung und gegen die Welt',
und daß seine vielbewunderte Solidarität mit seiner Mann-

schaft die Solidarität mit dem Volk gegen das Regime verstanden werden könnte."[14]

Although Karin exemplifies the individual who resists
being identified with a political creed, she does not
represent indifference to politics; if her invitation to
Karsch is in part an attempt to convince him that the
East Germans are still loyal to the ideal of a German
nation, she may also wish to convey to him her preference
for the form of government which is being put to the test
in the **Deutsche Demokratische Republik**, unfortunately under
the aegis of communist officials.   In both **Das dritte
Buch über Achim** und **Mutmaßungen über Jakob**, while exhibiting
his approval of characters who persevere in being guided
by their conscience rather than by political dogma, Johnson writes of actual political events and shows how his
characters' lives are affected by sociopolitical circumstances.   The reaction of the Russians and the East German
communists to the Hungarian revolution impinges on Jakob's
everyday activities and causes him to become suspicious
of the Ulbricht regime's respect for socialist principles.
Intruding on Jakob's perception of life in West Germany, the
Suez crisis confirms, it must be assumed, his doubts about
the good intentions of governments which call themselves
democratic and peace-loving.   In **Das dritte Buch über
Achim** the issue of German reunification is a significant
aspect of the background. Johnson has devoted a large part

68

of one of his Frankfurt lectures to the question of why
Germany has remained divided. In his view the fault lies
mainly with the West German government; for Adenauer and
his confederates, Johnson insists, the concept of a neutral
but unified Germany was anathema. The **Bundesrepublik** would
renounce neither its allies nor its currency. To the Russians and the East Germans, however, a Germany based
politically on the model of Austria would have been readily
acceptable. Karsch's willingness to visit the East and to
publicize Achim and the East German authorities' desire
that he write the biography indicate that interest exists
in the two factions in communicating with one another.
Achim is amenable to being interviewed at length. It is the
West German Karsch who comes to the conclusion that Achim
is too intent on participating in the production of his
biography to make the venture successful. The element of
compromise which alone could affect reunification and
bring about the publication of Achim's story is lacking.

In "Eine Reise wegwohin" the political event which
determines the conclusion of the **Novelle** is the Spiegel
affair which concerned the (of course) unauthorized publication of military secrets and the ensuing paranoia
on the part of the Bonn government. As a result of the
hyperbolic vigilance of the security police, Karsch's
apartment is ransacked; anti-communist sentiment in the
West also makes it difficult for him to make himself heard

in his espousal of the cause of compromise. Frustrated in the East and in the West, he leaves both Germanies and travels first to Italy and then to the United States. Since Johnson followed the same course on his journey, eventually settling in Sheerness, England, on Sheppey Island, perhaps Karsch can be presumed to have ended his wandering there, too.

The need for compromise which for Karsch, made itself felt on the political scene, exhibited itself in the matter of the style of **Das dritte Buch über Achim.** In shaping **Mutmaßungen über Jakob** so that it would duplicate and so present reality, that is, the truth, Johnson had chosen the procedure of using a multiplicity of narrative forms, which all but obfuscated the reader. The style of **Das dritte Buch über Achim** is, for the most part, reportorial, foreshadowing the unbroken narration which characterizes Johnson's next novel, **Zwei Ansichten.** Nevertheless, Johnson still avoids, for the sake of reproducing actuality, telling his story in a completely logical and chronological fashion: here and there the narrative past tense gives way to the present and indirect discourse to direct rather indiscriminately. Because of the device of the narrator's seeming to respond to a series of questions, Johnson relates the events of the novel as if he were expressing a series of impressions.[15] To counteract the vagueness which sometimes results from the inexactness of this kind of approach, Johnson continues to make use of the device, employed liberally in **Mutmaβungen über Jakob**, of detailing the physical world in which the characters move; for example, Achim's bicycle receives careful attention. In juxtaposing narrative and impressionistic sequences, Johnson loses as much as he gains. Durzak has described the net effect: "Dinghaftes, lebloses Geschehen wird durch Bilder mythisiert . . ."[16] **Das dritte Buch über Achim** is an analysis of what certain people think about themselves and the society in which they live rather than a story about them. In writing his next novel **Zwei Ansichten** Johnson avoided experimenting with sophisticated literary devices and relied on simple narration because the tale he chose to tell had as its focal point a political event, the meaning of which did not need to be expressed symbolically--the building of the Berlin wall on August 13, 1961; that coup d'état provided no occasion for ambiguity.

FOOTNOTES

[1]It is possible, because of Johnson's fondness for colorful names, but improbable, because of the crudity of the ironic implication, that the name Karsch is a combination of a tribute to Brecht, whose didactic stories about Herr K(euner) Johnson must have admired, and a word for a part of the human anatomy most often used scatologically; this interpretation of the name is presented without comment in the article "Mutmaβungen wurden Gewiβheit" by Marcel Reich-Ranicki in **Ueber Uwe Johnson.**

[2]Uwe Johnson, **Das dritte Buch über Achim** (Frankfurt am Main: Suhrkamp, 1961), p. 74 f. Further references to this edition will be given in the text.

[3]Johnson contends in **Begleitumstände**, p. 302, that he insisted on putting a comma after **Karsch** in order to confound the purists in grammatical matters who had berated him for the abandon he was wont to exhibit in punctuating his run-on sentences.

[4]Quoted in **Werkstattgespräche mit Schriftstellern,** ed. Horst Bienek (München: DTV, 1965, implemented 1967), p. 106.

[5]See **Begleitumstände**, p. 193: "Gewiβ redet Karsch mit seinen Partnern am Telefon . . . Und er hat nun einmal seinen Spaβ, den Leser beim Erzählen sehen zu lassen, wie

er an das Erzählte geraten ist und wie er es mit dem anstellt mit dem Erzählen. (Auch bekannt als das Döblinische Syndrom.)"

[6]Schwarz, **Der Erzähler Uwe Johnson**, p. 32. N.B. also one of the questions which head the book's different sections: "Deswegen bliebst du da? Blieb Karsch da?" (**Das dritte Buch über Achim**, p. 37).

[7]See Karl Migner, **Uwe Johnson: Das dritte Buch über Achim** (München: C. Oldenbourg, 1966), p. 37: "Dabei handelt es sich bei den Figuren Karsch und Karin weder um Charaktere noch um Typen. Lediglich ihre Funktion ist wichtig . . ."

[8]Hans Mayer, **Zur deutschen Literatur der Zeit** (Reinbek bei Hamburg: Rowohlt, 1967), p. 338.

[9]Cited in Manfred Durzak, **Der deutsche Roman der Gegenwart** (Stuttgart: Kohlhammer, 1971), p. 178.

[10]See Edward Diller, "Uwe Johnson's Karsch: Language as a Reflection of the Two Germanies," **Monatshefte**, 60:1 (Spring 1968), especially p. 37: "The language of West Germany centers on the concrete objects of a materialistic society while the changes in East Germany are rooted in the often repeated concepts of the state ideology."

[11]Durzak, **Der deutsche Roman der Gegenwart**, p. 213. See also Dieter Sturm, "Karschs Verwandlung" in **Ueber**

Uwe Johnson, p. 135:   "Karsch hat sich also in einen ganz durchschnittlichen, etwas versponnenen, etwas zögernden Menschen verwandelt, der eigentlich recht unpolitisch ist."

[12]See Leslie L. Miller, "Uwe Johnson's 'Jahrestage': The Choice of Alternatives," Seminar, 10:1 (February 1974), 51.

[13]R. Hinton Thomas and Wilfred van der Will, Der deutsche Roman und die Wohlstandsgesellschaft (Stuttgart: Kohlhammer, 1969), p. 148.

[14]Quoted, ibid., p. 137.

[15]See Migner, Uwe Johnson: Das dritte Buch über Achim, p. 98.

[16]Durzak, Der deutsche Roman der Gegenwart, p. 243.

CHAPTER 4

ZWEI ANSICHTEN: ESCAPE FROM COMMITMENT

Johnson has stated that the **Zwei Ansichten (Two Views)**
are just that in every sense of the word, views of a
physical landscape, abstract viewpoints, and differing
opinions.[1] In expressing them he has restricted himself to
the use of a narrative technique which foregoes the employment of such devices as multiple and unidentified
vantage points, tense shifts, and symbol complexes.[2]
The story concerning a rather shabby love affair is told in
a straightforward manner, with chapters dealing alternately with the point of view of each of the two protagonists as perceived by a narrator who makes a personal
appearance only in the book's closing episode. Johnson has
explained the unexpected simplicity of this structure as
having come about because of the nature of the material
which he is presenting and has protested that he adheres
to no theory on literary matters which he might attempt to
illustrate in his writing: "Ueber eine Poetik . . . ver-
füge ich nicht," he explains in **Begleitumstände** (p. 328).
Since the situation in each of his books dictates the manner of its telling (an inquest into a mysterious death,
curiosity about a West German's reaction to life in the
East), the format of **Zwei Ansichten** developed readily from
the book's premise. The passage in **Begleitumstände** affords
further insight: "Hier aber sind es lediglich 'Zwei An-

sichten', in der Hauptsache nur zwei Personen, deren Auf-
enthaltsorte, Handlungen, Auffassungen und Entschlüsse
streng auseinandergehalten sind. Es ist eben eine ein-
fachere Geschichte, großenteils sogar geeignet für das
traditionelle Verfahren, die Entwicklungen von Gefühlsregungen zu beschreiben." These pronouncements indicate,
however, that Johnson was far from indifferent to the
question of what the novelist's objectives are. On a television program for the Bavarian schools, broadcast in
1973, Johnson came close to committing himself to a definition of the novel: "One might also call the novel a
system of correlations," he proposed, "including the relation to social establishments or to the weather, to which
each individual has, after all, his own, intrinsic relations. What is intended is, in the end, a discussion with
the reader."[3] As a consequence of the shape which these
considerations and the material itself gave to **Zwei Ansichten**, the book came to represent Johnson's most read-
able story. Henry Hatfield has designated it "his most
gripping book."[4]

While telling a quasi-adventuresome love story, Johnson
nevertheless concentrates on his theme which delineates
the relationship between political event and personal conscience. Since Johnson has reached the conclusion that the
effect of vast political movements on the individual can
best be demonstrated by depicting the lives of little,

that is, ordinary people,[5] he has chosen to make his protagonists inconspicuous citizens of East and West Germany, respectively. Their anonymity is emphasized by the fact that Johnson has not named them; they are simply Mr. B. and Miss D. The supposition that B. must indicate the **Bundesrepublik**, where he lives, and D. must indicate the **Deutsche Demokratische Republik**, where she lives, is hard to avoid and generally assumed by critics and readers to be valid. Johnson, however, has protested that he would eschew such obvious symbolism and seems to favor the device of assigning his protagonists proper names, such as those used by the publishers of the English translation of **Zwei Ansichten**; in **Begleitumstände** he refers to Dietbert B(allhusen) and Beate (p. 407 and elsewhere). Their unheroic natures and their typicality are, despite Johnson's mock protestations, better characterized by the initials B. and D.

B., indicating the **Bundesrepublik**, is a more appropriate appelation for a young man in his mid-twenties who makes his home in West Germany and works there as a photographer without compunction. Once again, as in Johnson's previous novels, the character's occupation, to which considerable attention is paid, and how he engages in it are treated as aspects of his personality. The expensive cameras B. uses, as well as the costly sports car which plays an equally important part in his life, symbolize his and the West German passion for amassing possessions, the **Dinghaftigkeit** of life in the **Bundesrepublik.** The fact that he makes his living by selling to newspapers and magazines the pictures he has taken only for the possibility of their newsworthiness is a key to the shallowness of his viewpoint and the superficiality of his talent. In regard to his love affair with D. the same elements in his personality prevail. Having become acquainted with her by chance on a visit to East Berlin and having slept with her as a matter of course rather than as an expression of his feelings, he recalls upon his return to the West both her and the time they spent with one another only imperfectly. In the meantime he has purchased a new sports car which he cherishes to a greater degree than he does the memory of D. When it is stolen during a visit to Berlin, on which occasion he had intended casually to resume his friendship with D., he is vexed more by the loss of the automobile than by his failure to reestablish contact with her. B.'s emotional immaturity and indifference to political reality have been strictly dealt with by critics of Johnson's fiction. The range of opinions about him extends from mild disapproval (Hatfield: "a weak, dull fellow") to scorn (Schwarz: "Herr B. gehört zur 'Pepsi-Generation', ohne daß er deren Unbekümmertheit und Lebenshunger teilt").[6]

At the time of the publication of **Zwei Ansichten** reviewers in West Germany were particularly offended by

what they considered to be Johnson's flawed portrait of
the typical citizen of the **Bundesrepublik**. Their cause
for concern seems well-founded when the conclusions about
Mr. B. reached by the American literary critic Mark Boulby
are taken into consideration: "In the figure of Herr B.
Johnson presents an acid indictment of a self-deluded
and inauthentic society, founded upon commercialism and
cheapness of feeling and cut off from any genuine commitment or the possibility of that kind of natural human
encounter that might make moral experience and social
justice more than mere words."[7] Because of the many faults
in B.'s character Johnson provides ambiguous motivation for
his heroic deed, the rescue of Miss D. from the East after
the Berlin wall has been erected. In accord with his theme
that political events which they do not instigate affect
the lives of ordinary people, Johnson depicts how the
building of the wall has changed B. from a politically
indifferent West German into a politically responsive one.
Johnson describes the transition in this sentence: "Denn
es war bei dem Streit darum gegangen, daß die D. ihn für
politisch dumm hielt; und sie hatte in ihrem Brief ge-
schrieben, daß sie noch am Sonnabend vor der Sperrung
durch Westberlin gefahren und nicht ausgestiegen war, was er
für politisch dumm hielt" (p.36). By referring to the
quarrel which had occurred at the time of B. and D.'s
last meeting, Johnson has presented the view held by the

inhabitants of the **Deutsche Demokratische Republik** that their counterparts, the citizens of the **Bundesrepublik**, are politically naive, if not politically ignorant. Mr. B., in turn, upon learning that D. had made a deliberate choice to remain in the East, is uncomprehending and accepts it as his duty to disabuse all East Germans of their blind faith in a communist regime. The notion of bringing D. over the wall out of East Berlin comes to B. as a means of foiling the political strategy of the DDR. After having urged her by letter to leave East Germany, he is not altogether enthusiastic when she responds affirmatively. Unable to see himself as a rescuer leading his beloved to safety through barbed wire and mine fields, B. at first fails in his efforts to find an agency which would arrange her passage to freedom for (not too much) money. He stumbles upon an altruistic group of conspirators in a West Berlin pub who undertake at the risk of their lives and only for the reimbursement of their expenditures to plan and carry out D.'s escape (as they have the escape of others) to the West. At this point B.'s conscience comes slightly into play: "Er wollte aber etwas versucht haben zu Gunsten der D., sich nichts vorwerfen müssen" (p. 75). In this instance, Johnson has provided another example of the intrusion of sociopolitical circumstance on the private sphere and has indicated at the same time that the effect this exercise of political power (Johnson uses the un-

usual word "Staatsmacht" for the state) has on the individual is to make him or her aware of moral choices.

What for B. is a faint stirring of conscience, is for
D. a major crisis in the matter of her integrity.   Although approximately an equal number of pages in **Zwei
Ansichten** are devoted to B. and to D., she is indeed Johnson's protagonist, as Durzak, for example, has contended:
"Zweifelsohne ist die D. für Johnson die eigentliche Haupt-
person . . ."[8] Affording another instance of the close
relationship which, Johnson poses, exists between character
and occupation, Miss D.'s activity as a nurse and her
devotion to her calling demonstrate that she is a person of
sensibility and intelligence.   One of the reasons for her
ultimate decision to leave the **Deutsche Demokratische Republik** is the awareness she has that the conscientious-
ness which she exhibits in her work goes unrecognized in
the workers' state; like Jakob in **Mutmaßungen über Jakob**
she begins to doubt that the cause which the East German
government purports to advance is just, and D., whose allegiance to the Ulbricht regime has been apolitical, is
compelled eventually to engage in a poltical act.   Another
reason for her discontent with life in the East arises from
the loss of the small apartment which she has maintained
for herself to satisfy her need for privacy in spite of
governmental regulations forbidding this kind of bourgeois
luxury; her defiance of laws which produce regimentation

having been discovered, she is forced to share a room in the hospital's nurses quarters. In D. the individuality perseveres which B. has surrendered in order to conform to the pattern established by his fellow West Germans in their pursuit of goods and wealth. After the erection of the wall, which D. seems to regard initally as an appropriate political symbol, even if brings about personal inconvenience, she is confronted with the problem of judging those whose reaction to the wall is to flee and defect, when first someone she knows casually and then her younger brother, the only member of her family with whom she has a close relationship, choose escape over remaining in a country in which they have become imprisoned.

Her uneasiness about renewing her affair with B. is kept at first on the periphery of these events and ruminations. When B.'s letter arrives, suggesting that she might herself chance an escape to the West, she realizes that she does indeed have a choice to make, not so much because of her need to be with B.,[9] but rather because of her need to give expression to her convictions. Johnson makes a point of explaining how she became personally involved in the political situation: "Sie war damals, ohne daß sie es hätte anfangen merken, mehr und mehr Gefühlen ausgeliefert, wo früher Gewöhnung und Kenntnisse sie bewahrt hatten vor Mitleid" (p. 57). D.'s decision to accept the help of the daring group of people who will provide her with false papers and escort her in her disguise to freedom in Denmark comes about not because B. has created this escape route but because she wishes to renounce a country which, by building the wall, has doubted her capacity to make a morally well-founded choice. "Sie hatte unter diesem Staat gelebt wie in einem eigenen Land," Johnson establishes, "zu Hause, im Vertrauen auf offene Zukunft und das Recht, das andere Land zu wählen" (p. 25). In providing motivation for D.'s decision to leave her homeland, Johnson has drawn on his own experiences. While his passage from East to West Berlin took place before the advent of the wall, even that move was the result of a difficult choice on his part. In one of a series of essayistic pieces, collected under the title of **Berliner Sachen (About Berlin)**, Johnson explains the nature of his disillusionment with the East German regime: "Mancher Einzelne, der sich der neuen Gemeinschaft gerade als Individuum überantworten wollte, hatte nun zu erfahren, daß er gar nicht als Einzelner angesehen werde, sondern als Angehöriger einer Gruppe. Diese Gruppe aber waren die Eltern, Leute der alten, der aufgegebenen Zeit."[10] The sense that they have been betrayed in their effort to maintain their personal integrity impels both Johnson and his projection of himself in fiction, Miss D., to choose to leave a land in which the dream of a people's republic has turned into the nightmare of a Kafkaesque frustration myth.

Because D. has decided to live in West Berlin, intellectually but not physically removed from the East, her reunion with B., an event of symbolic import, does not take place. Impatient to assume ownership of the new sports car he has ordered to replace the stolen one, B. has left West Berlin and has flown to the city in West Germany where the automobile plant is located. Upon being informed subsequently that he has missed meeting D. upon her arrival from Denmark, he drives (in his newly acquired car) to West Berlin and is precipitously involved in an automobile accident, and as a result he is hospitalized. Because her landlady urges her at least to visit him, D. sees him briefly on his sickbed and then leaves to set out on the truly important venture of establishing a new life for herself, in which B. can have no part. This course of events symbolizes in a general way the relationship between the two Germanies in regard to the hope of reunification. Representing two points of view held by two peoples now concretely separated, the East Germans and the West Germans, so Johnson would seem to propose, are no longer capable of finding a common ground where they could hammer out the terms of an agreement binding together their divided nation. Like B. and D. they have no ties which bind them, but instead two divergent views of the wall which separates them.

In this light D. has learned to accept the inevitability of the wall and the incontrovertibility of the fact

that the Germanies have become too different in their
orientation to be reunited. In addition, D.'s attitude
expresses Johnson's approximation of a solution to this
dilemma, often found incorporated in his women characters.
In choosing exile in West Berlin, D. has avoided adherence
to the sociopolitical creed of either East or West; in
a way she has duplicated Karin's feat of maintaining her
integrity while living under a political system which
disallows it. Gesine Cresspahl's attempt to establish
in West Germany and elsewhere the private world of a "moral
Switzerland," where the machinations of politicians will
not compromise her principles, is to be extensively explored in Johnson's next and voluminous novel **Jahrestage.**
Boulby has offered an answer to the question which must
occur as to why Johnson suggests that women deal more
successfully than men with the problem of adapting a personal code of ethics to the pressures of the political
situation; "what arises here," Boulby contends, "is a
question of balance, its essence being the attainment of a
proper equilibrium between individual and collective . . .
The woman . . . is the contradictory sign of that frontier
that runs between East and West, but also between person
and citizen, self and collective, truth . . . and u n truth."
In her role as mother, woman is, of course, the essential
part of the social unit; at the same time she remains an
individual as one of the partners in the pairing on which

family life is based. Her personal and her public selves are therefore intertwined. Johnson seems to have persuaded himself that he can more truthfully deal with the confrontation between the individual's morality and the sociopolitical environment by choosing to make his most effective protagonist a woman. Feminine self-sufficiency is also represented in Johnson's work by the frequently used and affirmatively evaluated symbol of the cat, an animal whose independence is legendary.

The generally favorable reception of **Zwei Ansichten** in the East was countered by less approving reviews in the West because of Johnson's conciliatory attitude toward both sides in their opinions about the wall. One critic, Horst Krüger, took Johnson to task for his lack of moral probity, finding that his position on the matter of the wall was wavering: he sat "nicht diesseits, nicht jenseits der Mauer, sondern gewissermaßen auf der Mauer, mit nichts anderem befaßt, als beide Seiten zu Protokoll zu nehmen."[12] The depth of the Western disapproval of Johnson's stance was the result of a public debate about the wall in which Johnson became embroiled as an East German author who had achieved literary prominence by taking up residence in the West. Having been awarded a government grant and the use of a villa in Italy in order to be able to write at his leisure, Johnson became on November 11, 1961, part of a panel of authors and critics discussing literary matters

on the Italian radio. The German author and editor Hermann
Kesten, who was also a participant, spoke unkindly of some
East German institutions such as Bertolt Brecht and the
wall, and Johnson felt compelled to take issue with him.
In essence, Johnson defended himself against the charge
that he was morally pusillanimous in not being outraged
by the building of the "wall of shame." Responding in the
light of the literary principles to which he adhered, he
maintained that fiction was not the province of political
propaganda: "Ich meine nicht, daβ die Aufgabe der Literatur wäre die Geschichte mit Vorwürfen zu bedenken. Die
Aufgabe der Literatur ist vielmehr eine Geschichte zu
erzählen, in meinem Fall hieβe das, sie nicht auf eine
Weise zu erzählen, die den Leser in Illusionen hinein-
führt, sondern ihm zeigt, wie diese Geschichte ist."[13]
He had, however, prefixed to this statement some remarks
which lent themselves to misinterpretation: "Die ostdeutschen Kommunisten haben, als sie diese Mauer zogen,
nicht die Absicht gehabt, unmoralisch zu handeln, sondern
sie befanden sich in der Notwehr . . ." In the West German press Kesten turned the literary debate into a political free-for-all. Johnson made every effort to clarify
his position, but garnered only frustration which led him
to retreat more and more into privacy, the avoidance of
confrontation, and eventually into isolation. The protagonist in his next novel **Jahrestage** flees the scene of a

divided Germany to what she takes to be the moral ambiguity
of cosmopolitan New York City. The journal she keeps there,
nevertheless, gives clear evidence of her (and Johnson's)
continuing preoccupation with the sociopolitical dilemmas
of German life.

The relative clarity with which the two views are
presented is matched by the book's relative clarity in
style. Since the means by which the plot proceeds is anecdotal, presenting a series of incidents in the lives of
the two lovers, Johnson uses an almost reportorial prose
in relating these events. Engaged in telling a story
for the story's sake, he avoided composing a multilayered
text, wherein several vantage points intersect and the
narrative past tense is intermingled with the dramatic present to achieve **erlebte Rede**, a device which simulates
the immediacy of the sensations and alogical thinking.
Because Johnson still maintains that the author's goal
must be the reproduction of reality, the reader is still
burdened with the task of unraveling Johnson's paratactic
sentences, dumped into a paragraph's bottomless pit (one
paragraph is occasionally two pages long).[14] The vocabu-
lary is eclectic, ranging from punning (Ulbricht is **der
Sachwalter**) and dialectical expressions to the argot of
working class and professional people. The grammar which
holds together these disparate elements is unconventional,
more akin to English than to German grammar. In **Begleit-**

umstände Johnson has himself characterized these tendencies: "Eine Vorliebe für die Parataxe, eine Abneigung
gegenüber hypotaktischen Lösungen werden eingestanden,
desgleichen die Neigung, die Beziehungen zwischen Subjekt-
Prädikat-Objekt straff zu halten, demnach Adverbiales
außerhalb dieses Feldes nach-, auch vorzuliefern. Das hat
gelegentlich die Folge, daß das Verbum in zwei Bedeutungen
des Wortes 'vorgezogen' wird . . . Da ist die Absicht,
Sie [den Kritiker] auszulocken aus Ihren Lesegewohnheiten,
und erlaubt ist es obendrein."[15] Having been berated
for his leftist-leaning opinions, Johnson has been accused
not only of being a traitor to the cause of German nationhood but to the cause of the German language as well.

The most unremitting criticism of Johnson's prose
has been written by Karl-Heinz Deschner in **Talente, Dichter,
Dilettanten**, which labels Johnson's German the worst in
modern times in terms of style. His run-on sentences, as a
matter of fact, contain elements both of the traditional
basis of German prose--the Luther Bible--and of at least
two twentieth century masters--Fontane and Brecht. The
following passage from **Zwei Ansichten**, chosen at random,
may afford some insight into the sources, mannerisms, and
virtues of Johnson's writing.

> Sie war mit ihm zumeist im westlichen Berlin
> gewesen, sie allein konnte in der Erin-
> nerung dahin zurück, wieder mit bloßen
> Füßen ratlos inmitten aufgeschlagner Schuh-
> kartons sitzen, wieder mit dem Finger auf

> die fremden Waren in den vollgestopften
> Vitrinen des Kramladens zeigen, immer noch
> einmal im selben Juniwind an einem ver-
> schwenderisch mit bunten Zeitungen behäng-
> ten Kiosk stehen und die reißerischen
> Schlagzeilen lesen, zwar als stehe sie ein
> paar Schritte weg und beobachte sich; jedoch
> in der Vorstellung, da mit ihm zu sein,
> bleichten die äußeren Kennzeichen des
> Westens aus und wurden überdeckt von Fassa-
> denfarben, Autoformen, Bahnbrückenhöh-
> len diesseits der Grenze, meist der Um-
> gebung ihres verlorenen Zimmers, und zwar
> bei naßkaltem, vorwinterlichem Wetterlicht;
> so konnte sie sich auch einbilden, sie führe
> B., seinen befangenen Schritt neben sich,
> durch die Korridore des Krankenhauses und
> erkläre ihm die Stationen, er hatte sie
> aber nie abgeholt, nur einmal gesagt in
> einem lustlosen, pflichtschuldigen Ton:
> Das mußt du mir mal alles zeigen (p. 90).

The number of paratactical constructions is overwhelming;
the rhythm of the selection is that of the Bible. Although the use of the extended participial construction
("an einem verschwenderisch mit bunten Zeitungen behängten
Kiosk"), by which Johnson pays homage to Fontane, indicates
sophistication, the general tone is conversational, particularly in the choice of words: e.g., "vollgestopft,"
"immer noch einmal," "aufgeschlagne(r) Schuhkartons" and
in the positioning of the verb: "die äußeren Kennzeichen
des Westens . . . wurden überdeckt von Fassadenfarben,
Autoformen, etc." The Brechtian lyricism, compounded of
functional cityscapes ("Vitrine," "Kramladen," "Kiosk,"
"Schlagzeile") and poetic neologisms (e.g., "bei naß-
kaltem, vorwinterlichem Wetterlicht") gives the ordinary

the import of the mythic. (The influence of the style of the Grimms' **Märchen** must also be considered.) This manner of writing lends itself to Johnson's attempt to reproduce everyday reality, by which the destiny of the common lot, people with no political power, is determined, and yet the same style gives his individuality ample room. The combination of the social and the personal is appropriate to the theme of his work, the interaction between private conscience and public event. In **Der deutsche Roman und die Wohlstandsgesellschaft**, the authors relate this juxtaposition to Johnson's inclination to satirize the conventional, politically naive novel: "Johnsons Stil, der Distanz zur Sprache der Propaganda wahrt, die der Autor glaubt, entlarven und verspotten zu können, kann als eine Diktion der ideologischen Ernüchterung beschrieben werden."[16] In Johnson's next and last lengthy novel **Jahrestage**, style and story directly reflect one another; shorn of its mannerisms while retaining the vigor of its depiction of the confrontation between the sociopolitical and intimate worlds, Johnson's prose reaches a new height of subtlety; unfortunately, it proceeds at a snail's pace (Johnson is supposed to have written about a page a day) on what would be a trip around the equator.

FOOTNOTES

[1] Uwe Johnson, **Begleitumstände**, p. 326: "Entsprechend meint der Titel auch die alten Bedeutungen des Wortes
Ansicht, die vue, den Prospekt, 'von meiner Seite her ge-
sehen', bis hinzu schlichte Verschiedenheit der Meinungen."

[2] See Bernd Neuman, **Utopie und Mimesis** (Kronberg:
Athenäum, 1978), p. 14: "'Zwei Ansichten' (1965) haben
keinerlei Spuren der Johnsonschen Begegnung mit Faulkner."

[3] Quoted in **Motives**, Richard Salis, ed., Egon Larsen,
trans. (London: Oswald Wolff, 1975), p. 106.

[4] Henry Hatfield, **Crisis and Continuity in Modern
German Fiction** (Ithaca and London: Cornell University
Press, 1969), p. 150.

[5] See Uwe Johnson, **Zwei Ansichten** (Reinbek bei Hamburg:
Rowohlt, 1968), "Auskünfte und Abreden zu 'Zwei Ansichten,'"
p. 117: "Ich bin überzeugt, daß die 'einfachen Leute'
das erheblichere Beispiel abgeben für Lebensverhältnisse
in unserer Zeit . . ." Johnson repeats the quotation in
Begleitumstände, p. 329. Further references to this edition will be given in the text.

[5] Schwarz, **Der Erzähler Uwe Johnson**, p. 35; Hatfield,
Crisis and Continuity in Modern German Fiction, p. 154.

[7] Boulby, **Uwe Johnson**, p. 81.

[8] Durzak, **Der deutsche Roman der Gegenwart**, p. 227.

[9]Hatfield's contention in **Crisis and Continuity in Modern German Fiction**, p. 158: "She is genuinely in love with B. . . .," is an assumption resulting from a reading of **Zwei Ansichten** as romantic fiction, a direction Johnson has somewhat encouraged his readers to take by noting in his answers to Schoelman's questions similarities between his and other Romeo and Juliet stories.

[10]Johnson, **Berliner Sachen**, p. 54.

[11]Boulby, **Uwe Johnson**, p. 60 f.

[12]Horst Krüger, "Das verletzte Rechtsbewußtsein" in **Ueber Uwe Johnson**, p. 143.

[13]Johnson, **Begleitumstände**, p. 215. Johnson quotes himself.

[14]The poet and critic Michael Hamburger poses the possibility that Johnson's convoluted prose may be evidence of the fact that he was an alcoholic: "Hamburger often saw," a newspaper report states, "how Johnson, unable to write following his alcoholic excesses helplessly pondered over sentences and surrounded himself with a 'wall of intransigence. He was bound to destroy himself,'" quoted in **The German Tribune**, Dec. 9, 1984 (No. 1159), p. 10.

[15]Johnson, **Begleitumstände**, p. 188.

[16]Thomas and van der Will, **Der deutsche Roman und die Wohlstandsgesellschaft**, p. 147.

CHAPTER 5

JAHRESTAGE: COMMITMENT TO A MORAL SWITZERLAND

Heinz D. Osterle has pointed out the experimental nature of **Jahrestage**:[1] it is a unique work in the field of the novel, consisting of almost two thousand pages of text, published as four separate books.[2] The division into four parts is more incidental than pertinent because Johnson has established at the outset that **Jahrestage** (first working title: **Anniversarii**) will consist of a series of journal entries beginning on August 20, 1967, and ending on August 20, 1968. As the subtitle "Aus dem Leben von Gesine Cresspahl" indicates, this record of the events in her life and her ruminations on them is both autobiographical and biographical: "von" means both "by" and "about." The relationship between the author and his protagonist is, accordingly, subtle, at the very least to the extent that the circumstances dealt with in the novel reflect Johnson's own experiences during a prolonged stay in New York City (from 1966 to 1968), while his protagonist--a woman--is his creation, yet functions independently in the book. On a few occasions Gesine and Johnson appear together on the pages of **Jahrestage**: e.g., "Wer erzählt hier eigentlich, Gesine. Wir beide. Das hörst du doch, Johnson."[3] The days of the year are scrutinized from three vantage points: as Gesine experiences them in the present, working in a bank in New York, becoming involved in a rela-

tionship with D. E., **ein deutscher Emigrant** from Mecklenburg, who wants to marry her, and attending to the upbringing of her ten-year-old daughter Marie; then as she
takes time to reflect and dwell on the past, on the lives
of her parents and relatives and on her own life as a child
and young woman, growing up and going to school during the
grim years of Germany's collapse. In addition, Johnson has
assembled for the pages of **Jahrestage** a vast amount of
material excised from the the New York **Times**, which he has
translated verbatim or reproduced in substance. These
passages, Johnson has been careful to note, have been selected "subjectively, with the eyes of Mrs. Cresspahl. . ."[4]
Therefore, they represent yet another element in her life,
its sociopolitical aspect, taking on the features of a
maiden aunt, whose function it is to set standards for all
of society--"unsere gute alte Tante, gerecht, hilfsbereit,
die ethische Gallionsfigur" (II, 609). This combination of
narrative levels, each of which is elaborately explored,
produces a work of what must be judged to be excessive
le.ng'th--the number of characters is so overwhelming that a
guide has been provided to sort them out: **Kleines Adreß-
buch für Jerichow und New York, Ein Register zu Uwe Johnsons Roman Jahrestage**, edited by Rolf Michaelis (Frankfurt
am Main: Suhrkamp, 1983). The novel's complexity and
longwindedness afford it stature as an experiment in the
epic form the object of which is to reconstruct, in John-

son's words, "die Wirklichkeit jenes Jahres 1967/68 wie sie gerade komme, auf die Gefahr hin binnen eines Jahrzehnts darzustehen mit Kapiteln unfunktionell gewordener Tages- oder Zeitereignisse, wenn auch mit den so gewonnenen Hinweis, mit welch belanglosem und belastendem Schutt eine Person des zwanzigsten Jahrhunderts sich abzugeben habe Tag für Tag."[5] Both the grandeur of the enterprise and Johnson's doubts about the possiblity of attaining his goal are exhibited in the quotation. While readers of **Jahrestage** may not be able to avoid becoming bored with the mass of details which is used to shore up the novel's true-to-life dimensions and critics may cavil,[6] the book is destined to become a significant part of the literary legacy of the West; **Die Zeit** has recently put it on its list of the one hundred great books in world literature.

The novel's principal protagonist Gesine Cresspahl represents the third stage of development in Johnson's analysis of modern man in contention with the sociological and political aspects of his destiny. Jakob, Karsch, and perhaps B. have been sequestered in disillusionment, the primary state of mind resulting from the realization that they are powerless to change the course of human events, even to the extent that they might at least maintain their own integrity. Having reached a point of stasis, Jakob half-consciously strays into the path of a train; Karsch leads a meaningless life in exile; and B. accepts a rela-

tionship with a sports car as a substitute for another
human being. (It is ironic that Johnson himself lived out
the last years of his life in a stage of dismal disillusionment caused by the failure of his marriage.)   On
the other hand, D., whom B. failed to appreciate, Karin, and
the Gesine of the **Mutmaßungen über Jakob** all have the capacity to effect a compromise in the struggle between conscience and political reality; they learn that individuality can persevere against the forces of conformism by
way of accommodating themselves to the existing situation,
by making use of it, or by contending with it in a place
where choice is still a viable factor.   This second phase
of dealing with stressful life in the twentieth century
is an advance beyond the fatalism which characterizes Jakob's reaction to the discovery of his helplessness. At the
end of **Jahrestage** Gesine, so it would seem, has cast aside
the remnants of passivity which still remain in the second
stage of the individual's search for fulfillment and has
set out to contribute to the establishment of a socialist
utopia in Czechoslovakia.   The plot of **Jahrestage** traces
Gesine's odyssey as she she seeks out a moral Switzerland,
a country in which the individual conscience can thrive,
released from the constraints of political oppression.

    The destiny which sends Gesine off on her quest has
its origins in the lives of her parents; each contributes
in a particular way to the fashioning of her individualis-

tic personality. Lisbeth (nee Papenbrock), Gesine's mother, provides her daughter with an example of religious fervor, devotion to a cause to the point of martyrdom. She is the only one of Johnson's "plain people" whose activism has heroic dimensions. Having accepted the doctrine of man- kind's sinfulness, she seeks to atone for the guilt she feels at first for her own actions and then for the actions of the community. From her point of view she has erred in pursuing Cresspahl, who has become interested in her, because her family expects her to marry another man. With- out the knowledge of her parents she has visited Cresspahl in England, where he manages a business, before their wed- ding can take place. Her sense that she has failed her parents once more and her country and herself as well by returning to Richmond in England to begin married life in a kind of exile causes her to flee back to Germany to await the birth of her and Cresspahl's first child, the product of a relationship which is of the flesh and therefore inherently impure. When her husband relinquishes a good livelihood as a cabinetmaker in England and his hope for a life in a democratic society in order to establish a home for his wife and child in the German town of Jerichow where Lisbeth's family lives, she only finds herself burdened with the additional guilt of having ruined his life in addition to her own. To recompense in part those close to her for the injury she has inflicted by way of removing

herself from their lives, she attempts suicide. Frustrated
in carrying out this sinner's auto-de-fe, she resorts to
psychopathic measures in making no move to save her daughter
from drowning when she falls into a filled rain-barrel:[7] she
intends, so Johnson implies, to spare Gesine the suffering
which the flesh is heir to. Rescued by her father, Gesine
is subjected to yet another kind of rite of purification
when her mother decides not to give her enough to eat. What
Gesine learns, as, now an adult, she reflects on her mother's
aberrations, is that she can understand the passion and the
torment behind the religious fanatic's sense of justice.

Lisbeth's mission to execute God's justice on earth--
one is reminded of the many characters in Friedrich Dürrenmatt's plays who are also self-appointed avenging angels--
begins to have political dimensions when the Nazis rise to
power in Germany. She becomes a reluctant participant in
a trial by means of which the Nazis intend to dispose of one
of their opponents; she finds that she can as little contribute to the triumph of justice on the public scene as in
the private sphere. Gradually she has to concede that her
family and her country, devotion to which she has placed
above her personal happiness, have been corrupted by their
involvement with an evil regime. History itself forces
her to make a public demonstration of her anti-Nazi senti-
ments when at the time of the infamous **Kristallnacht** she
witnesses the abuse of the Jewish community in Jerichow

and attempts to intervene on their behalf. Subsequently, because of her failure as an individual and a member of the populace, she determines to perform the symbolic act of self-immolation and during the absence of her husband and daughter sets fire to the part of their home in which she has incaserated herself. Although the fire is discovered and extinguished before the building is completely destroyed, she dies in her funeral pyre's heat and fumes, a martyr in the fight against evil. In recalling the events of her mother's life which she can, of course, only remotely have been aware of (so that at this point Johnson becomes co-author of her journal), Gesine cannot fail to recognize that she has inherited her mother's compelling need to maintain her sense of integrity, to be able to live with a clear conscience. Fortunately for her, this trait, which tends to express itself in extreme fashion, is balanced by a pragmatic and conciliatory temperament which is her father's contribution to her personality.

Although Heinrich Cresspahl has been an important, if enigmatic figure in **Mutmaßungen über Jakob**, the human dimensions of his character are realized only in **Jahrestage**, where he represents a unifying element since the events of his life span the three sociopolitical epochs covered in the novel—the years of the Weimar Republic and its experiment with socialism, the dark era of totalitarianism and war, and the time of chaos and a divided Germany, which he lives out in Soviet imprisonment and then behind East Germany's wall and barricades. Cresspahl is also unusual among the figures in Johnson's novels in that he is portrayed as having an active part in politics. A member of the Socialist Party as a young man, he has become disillusioned with the role political parties play in establishing governmental policy; he learns to detest the equivocation which prevails among politicians of all persuasions. Unhappy with the course the Socialist Party has taken in the Weimar years, Cresspahl is eager to enter upon an apprenticeship beyond Germany's borders. Eventually, he decides to settle in Richmond, England, where he can aspire to having his own cabinetmaker's shop and is content with the more consistently democratic processes which undergird Britain's political structure. Personal ties bring him back to Germany in the end, where he tries to insulate himself and his family against the ruinous and pervasive influence of the Nazi regime. His wife's suicide then forces him to realize that the attempt to remain aloof from the problems which beset society must fail. In reaction, he undertakes to use political circumstances to his own advantage. Although he applies for membership in the Nazi Party, an affiliation which would assure him of assignments in his vocation, he avoids carrying the process to completion. He later assists in the building of a Luftwaffe base in the vicinity of Jerichow, but manages to

confine his construction activities to the housing build-
ings accessory to the actual military installations. In
describing Cresspahl's involvement in these matters and in
his later undercover work for the British intelligence, Johnson is conspicuously and perhaps necessarily vague (he could
have had little concept of how adults acted clandestinely
in these years); it is, however, not his accomplishment but
his attitude toward these political events as they intrude
on his well-buttressed integrity which impresses the child
Gesine and affects her character. From her father she learns
the art of survival, of keeping one's head above the murky
political waters, of outwitting and outlasting the regimes
of tyrants.

In this deadly serious game of contention between the
inidividual and amoral, if not immoral social and governmental forces, Cresspahl is called upon to test his mettle
particularly after the defeat of Hitler's Germany. Having
been a quasi-secret agent for the British in the last years
of the war, he becomes the choice of the English occupying
forces to be mayor of Jerichow. When the Russians take over
administration of the area, Cresspahl continues in his post,
although, in the eyes of the townspeople, he has betrayed
Germany in assisting the invaders by remaining mayor. Of
course, he has not taken up the Russian cause, but has once
again provided a pragmatic answer to the question of how
the individual can resist oppression: Cresspahl ameliorates

the harsh conditions imposed on the community by the Communist occupying powers. His (successful) efforts to provide a girl raped and impregnated by Russian soldiers with an abortion lead to the collapse of his stratagem; he is removed from office, arrested, and imprisoned as an enemy of the deliverers of Germany. In describing the tortures which Cresspahl undergoes in the hands of his Communist keepers, Johnson most probably is imagining the circumstances under which his own father died in Russian captivity. For Gesine the loss of her father is temporary but has just as permanent an effect. Having seen the results of an unrelenting devotion to the cause of conscience on her mother's part, Gesine now finds that she must resist with equal vigor choosing for herself the opposite role of the political activist. Despite her espousal of the socialist form of governance she leaves East (and then again West) Germany; despite her liberal views she remains aloof from American politics, letting their reality reach her only after having been filtered through the sedate pages of the New York **Times**, thus a reality colored by the paper's humanistic toleration. Gesine's lonely search for a position of compromise, somewhere between the ideals of Christian ethics and the heroism or martyrdom of a soldier on the political battlefield, is foreshadowed in her father's fate. Eventually exonerated (in a fashion) and freed, he returns to Jerichow a broken man who lives on for his

daughter's sake: for her and because of the need to provide her with an education under an anti-Nazi government
(even though an equally fascistic one), he remains in East
Germany; in order not to become a burden to her, he stays
behind when she flees to the West. Her inheritance from
him is his philosophy of thinking independently: "Er
brachte es ihr bei: Was ich sehe, was ich höre, was ich
weiß, es ist allein meines . . . Es ist nicht schlecht zu
lügen; solange die Wahrheit geschützt wird. Es ist lustig,
daß alle anderen Kinder es anders lernen; es ist nicht
gefährlich. Wir haben eine andere Wahrheit, jeder seine"
(II, 856).

Gesine Cresspahl is obviously Johnson's favorite character;[8] she is his amanuensis, and he hers. As a fictitious personage, she can give expression to the ideal which
Johnson cherishes of the totally free individual. **Jahrestage** traces her progress toward the realization of that kind
of self-fulfillment; it ends with the goal in sight--but
perhaps still unattainable.[9] Gesine's own involvement with
sociopolitical forces begins, as did Johnson's, during
adolescence, at the time of her father's imprisonment.
Her acceptance of her role as a member of the community
is withdrawn on the basis of the fact that its leaders
have perpetrated or at least acquiesced in an injustice;
Gesine even refuses to talk to the minister Wilhelm Brüs-
haver, whom the Nazis had sent to a concentration camp

because of his condemnation of them in his sermon delivered
during her mother's funeral service. She believes him guilty
of complicity with the Communists in bringing about her
father's arrest. Although Gesine is reconciled with Brüs-
haver upon her father's release from imprisonment, her
relationship with the church never loses the aspect of the
tenuous; equally so is her inclination to approve of the
East German government, especially in the light of the
socialism it purports to advance. That tentative allegiance is abandoned as soon as Gesine learns of the official
approbation afforded Stalin's antisemitic policies in Russia. Through these confrontations with political event,
as well as by the effect upon her of the diverse examples
set for her by her parents, she comes to conclude that she
must develop her own standards and create her own political
philosophy.

As much as she is the non-conformist in regard to her
activities in community life, she is also the confirmed
outsider in her relationship with her schoolmates and peers.
During her pre-university years in school, a period covered
by Johnson in excessive detail, Gesine finds only two
friends, both of whom are free spirits, without affiliation.
Robert Pagenkopf, nicknamed Pius, joins Gesine in her outsider status since he is the only Catholic in the class;
they soon arrange to sit beside one another in a remote
corner of the room, not adhering to the usual seating

arrangements; looked upon by the other students as a couple in love with one another, they regard themselves rather as brother and sister who share a common background and disposition. They are co-conspirators in the printing and distribution of broadsides satirizing the pretension of the Ulbricht regime to democratic objectives. Because he can neither break with the society in which he has his roots nor become a bona fide member of it, Pius elects to seek anonymity in the people's army, where his individualism persists to the degree that he takes on the assignment of test pilot, an occupation compatible with outsider tendencies. He is killed in a crash (as is subsequently D. E., another of Gesine's protectors). In the meantime Gesine has found a substitute brother-and-sister relationship with Jakob Abs, who has entered her life as a refugee in Jerichow at the end of the war. The second of her schoolday companions, Anita Grantlik, conforms to the pattern of unorthodoxy which Gesine and Pius have established for themselves. Deserted by her father, raped and infected with disease by Russian soldiers, she finds refuge neither among the occupied nor the occupiers in East Germany; her survival is the result of her own efforts. Because she cannot in good conscience stand by while an oppressive regime abuses the people of her country, even though she has severed her ties with it, she participates in the activities of the political underground, together with Gesine and

Pius. Later, after the erection of the Berlin wall, she
assists in the smuggling out of East Germans to the West--
to add to the novel's realism, Johnson pretends that he must
cast some doubt on Anita's participation in this venture,
in order to help conceal the identity of any and all "ene-
mies of the state." Afterwards, Anita defects to the West
herself. Anita's friendship with Gesine turns out to be
the one abiding, extra-familial relationship in Gesine's
life. She lends Gesine support during every crisis in her
restless life and makes appropriate arrangements to assure
Gesine's success in her endeavor--possibly her last act of
good conscience--to provide financial stability (through the
agency of the bank for which she works) for the democratic government in Czechoslovakia.

Although Gesine does not take part in the worker and
student uprising in East Berlin on June 17, 1953, she makes
use of the occasion of its suppression to come to the
decision to leave for the West. The personal element in
arriving at this resolve is not lacking, since she has, in
the previous year, been subjected to arrest and interroga-
tion at the hands of the East German security police, who
were preparing a case against a member of the student underground movement. Released herself after several days of
imprisonment, she has subsequently witnessed the trial
of her former fellow-student and the suspected insurgent,
Dieter Lockenvitz, and has heard her beaten and humiliated

friend sentenced to fifteen years of imprisonment. Leaving behind her father, who, she is aware, approves of her acting independently, and her "brother" Jakob, who has given his allegiance to the state, and leaving unfinished her studies at the university in Halle, Gesine crosses the border to West Germany. In the Rhineland she attends a school for translators and soon finds employment with the Nato organization. The events which impinge on her existence at this juncture are related in the earlier novel **Mutmassungen über Jakob**.

Johnson continues her story in **Jahrestage**, at a time when Gesine has been living for several years in New York City with her ten-year-old daughter Marie (Jakob is the child's father, as the reader soon becomes aware). Shortly after Marie's birth in West Germany, which occurs after her father's death in the **Deutsche Demokratische Republik** (the central event in **Mutmaβungen über Jakob**), Gesine has decided that if she becomes occupied with with some or any aspect of the monetary system which, she believes, represents the sociopolitical world's most trenchant intrusion on the private sphere, she will be able to exercise at least some control over her own and Marie's destiny. She has, therefore, studied (studying is the German solution to all problems) banking and found work with an insitution in Düsseldorf, and it has sent her in the spring 'of 1961 to its New York branch office. In an ironic turn of events,

Gesine's effort to have some, even if a remote influence
on the sources of power is temporarily frustrated when she
allows her conscience to interfere with her plans: she
warns a customer of the bank against entering into a transaction which would serve the bank's and not her (the customer's) interests; consequeently Gesine is dismissed. After
a difficult period of unemployment, she finds another position in banking, that of a secretary proficient in foreign
languages, because, in a twist of the plot which compounds
the irony, the chief officer of the bank is impressed by
her willingness to be truthful about the firing. In accord
with Gesine's calculations, albeit rather unexpectedly,
her new position turns out to be a stepping stone to one
which affords her the opportunity to have a part in the
political process. Her employer, de Rosny, undertakes
to provide the socialist country of Czechoslovakia, for
the moment relatively free of Russian domination, with a
loan to help sustain its independence; Gesine is not only
the appropriate (she has studied the Czech language) and
immediately available person who can bring de Rosny's plans
to fruition, she is also best suited personally to carry
out the bank's mission since its cause is one to which she
is already devoted. In this venture, which, not incidentally, is to the advantage of the bank and the American government, the moral act and political reality intersect; Gesine can assist in laying the foundations for her "moral

Switzerland," where the individual can live with a clear conscience, untroubled by the fear that political and social forces will infect him with their immorality--or, at least, amorality. The political message of **Jahrestage** can be garnered from this course of events.

It is the function of the four volumes of **Jahrestage** to explore the relationship between the individual and society, which is both the individual's point of origin and the result of an aggregate of individuals. Ostensibly a journal, meant for Marie's perusal, recording Gesine's memories of the past and observations about the present during the days of one year, from August 20, 1967, to August 20, 1968, the novel makes clear, almost from the beginning, what Gesine's intentions are. She describes to D. E., another German living in exile in the United States who has become her protector and (occasional) lover, her purposes in providing Marie with this personal history: "Aber was sie [Marie] wissen will ist nicht Vergangenheit, nicht einmal ihre. Für sie ist es eine Vorführung von Möglichkeiten, gegen die sie sich gefeit glaubt, und in einem andern Sinn Geschichten" (I, 144). Juxtaposed with Gesine's account of her own and her family's history[10] are extensive quotations (sometimes in summary) from the pages of the New York **Times**. The inclusion in a novel of previously printed journalistic material appears as a literary device in the work of Alfred Döblin--notably in **Berlin Alexanderplatz**--

and specifically in the form of newspaper headlines and leads
in John Dos Passos's U.S.A. trilogy; both authors, as Johnson has acknowledged, have received his attention.[11]   In
Jahrestage these newspaper excerpts, chosen, so Johnson has
insisted, to suit Gesine's purposes,[12] represent the American sociopolitical environment, with particular emphasis on
its New York aspect.   (The objection has been raised that
Johnson provides Gesine with no cultural experiences at
all: Gesine rarely mentions attending the theater, a mu-
sical event, or visits a museum or finds this kind of experience stimulating enough to deserve comment).   The abun-
dance of this documentary material all but turns the **Times**
into a person in the novel; Gesine herself feels compelled
to see the paper every day and characterizes it as a "correct" maiden aunt, "unsere gute alte Tante, gerecht, hilfsbereit, die ethische Gallionsfigur" (II, 609).   This quasi-
personage confronts Gesine, the confirmed individualist, with
the faceless society whose existence threatens to engulf
her own.   The societal and political problems which beset
the United States are regarded with concern but with humanistic detachment by America's leading newspaper, and thus
Gesine is called upon to reflect on such general difficulties
as crime on the streets and in the subways of New York
City, the prejudicial treatment of American blacks, anti-
war demonstrations and such specific catastrophies as the
murders of Martin Luther King and Robert Kennedy.   On all

these occurrences Gesine casts a cold eye and refuses to let them cause her to lose control of her life. She does react to the extent that she chooses not to become a member, especially a politically active one, of the society which contends with these ills; pointedly, she declines to take part in an anti-Vietnam war march in Washington, D.C., although she personally believes in its objectives. She clings to the hope that she will be able to leave the United States and live elsewhere, in some "moral Switzerland," and declines to marry D. E., who can provide her with a home in his adoptive country and assume the role of father to Marie. In juxtaposing material from the **Times** and Gesine's reminiscences of her father's life in Weimar Germany, her parents' and relatives' experiences in Nazi Germany, her own and her friends' misadventures in post-war, divided Germany, Johnson makes an implicit comparison between those events and the events described in the articles in the **Times**. He has indicated, however, that no direct parallels between happenings in Germany and in the United States are to be drawn: "Es habe eben zu dem gemeinsamen Plan gehört, die Wirklichkeit jenes Jahres 1967/68 in diese Auswahl aus dem Leben von Gesine Cresspahl aufzunehmen, wie sie gerade komme . . ."[13] The problems inherent in American politics, although they are presented in great detail in **Jahrestage**, do not affect Gesine's course of action as the political machinations of the Nazis and the European com-

munists have; rather, since Gesine's journal is written
for Marie's perusal, they are offered as a subject of study
for the girl, who is being directed away from open political commitment.

Although Marie is the center of Gesine's attention
and her activities help shape the plot, such as it is, of
the novel, the character exists in large part as a foil
for Gesine in her ruminations. As a ten-year-old, Marie is
uncomfortably precocious, lacking the naivete and spontane-
ity of adolescence.[14] Her weekend excursions to Staten
Island with her mother by way of a trip on the ferry have
the unjoyousness of the routine. Her friends are adults;
instead of a visit to the zoo or an outing with her class-
mates, she participates in the ransoming and freeing of
Karsch, the protagonist in **Das dritte Buch über Achim**, who
reappears in **Jahrestage** as a captive of the Mafia. It is
the early development of political consciousness in Marie
which makes Gesine take the cautionary measure of keeping
a journal for her, which is to provide her with an alternative **Weltanschauung** to that of her peers. Undaunted and
exhibiting some of her mother's independence, Marie has
not only adopted the United States as her homeland but has
also accepted as her own the point of view of the American
liberal. She condemns intellectually the segregation of
the blacks but feels ill-at-ease when Francine, the "token"
black child in her class at (a Roman Catholic) school, spends

several days in the Cresspahl apartment. She is captivated
by the opulent way of life which de Rosny, her mother's
superior at the bank and a capitalist grandee, pursues.
The somewhat dutiful affection she has for her mother is
surpassed by her love and concern for D. E., as she calls
him (his name is Dietrich Erichson), her mother's most
loyal friend and suitor. When he is killed, rather gratu-
itously in terms of the plot, in an airplane crash, Gesine,
with the help of Anita, goes to elaborate lengths to keep
the news from her daughter. Like Gesine an exile from East
Germany, D. E. furnishes the example of an alternative
to the role of outsider and nonconformist which Gesine has
chosen to play. Having turned his back on the European
concerns of ethnic hatreds and political party warfare,
the wounds of war and the feelings of guilt, D. E. has committed himself to living and working in the United States
and is employed as a professor of physics who works at times
for a governmental agency. Marie can more readily adjust
to his idea of rectitude than to her mother's grudging
acceptance of New York as a place of refuge. Paul Konrad
Kurz has identified Marie's unquestioning admiration for
D. E. in his rejection of the past as "a form of youthful
emotional ethics."[15] But she also has inherited and expresses her mother's persistence in striving to maintain
her integrity in regard to her sociopolitical position;
Marie, too, has her file of items for the New York **Times**.

Marie is, of course, frustrated in her endeavor to see her mother married to D. E. and to enter upon a conventional family life in the United States; instead, she accompanies her mother on her trip to Czechoslovakia, where under a socialist and supposedly liberal government she will be able to keep both her independence and a clear conscience, un- encumbered by a sense of guilt for having acquiesced in the waging of war and the perpetuation of the evil of po- litical machinations. Apparently, at least for the reader knowledgeable in matters of European history, Gesine's suc- cess in providing Marie an opportunity to live in a socialist Switzerland (liberated Czechoslovakia), where political and personal morality are inseparable, will be of short--very short--duration. Deliberately, perhaps, Johnson does not afford his readers an ending to the **Jahrestage**, except in regard to the date. Gesine and Marie only stand on the threshold of the promised land, unaware that Russian tanks are already poised to sweep across the borders of their utopia.

No doubt expressing Johnson's own concept of the ef- fect he would wish his four-volume novel to have on the reader, Gesine at one point puts succinctly her thoughts about the book's message: "Jeder wird seine Schlüsse selber ziehen mussen, auf seine eigene Verantwortung" (IV, 1442).[16] According to remarks made in an interview with Manfred Durzak, Johnson has, nevertheless, indicated the direction

in which he wishes the reader to turn in drawing conclusions
about the purpose he (and Gesine) had in mind as he com-
piled the entries in her journal; Durzak summarizes in this
fashion: "So ist denn auch das registrierende Material
filternde Bewußtsein Gesines nur äußerlich zentral, wich-
tiger ist auf die Aufarbeitung der Vergangenheit gerichtet,
ihr Bewußtsein als moralische Instanz, als Suche danach,
wie man leben sollte . . ."[17] Johnson seems to have devoted almost two thousand pages to the exposition of the
relationship between the individual and society, of the
conflict between personal morality and public policy, while
remaining neutral and refraining from propaganda on behalf
of a particular solution.

In Johnson's last work of fiction, **Skizze eines Verunglückten**, a terse autobiographical account, couched in
allegory, of his problem-ridden life in the years when he
was trying to finish **Jahrestage**, he describes the tenor
of the fiction written by his protagonist, Joachim de
Catt (and likewise the tenor of his own): "Auch er habe
sich bemüht, einzelne Personen mir zu zeigen in ihrem Zusammenhang mit mehreren, in der Einrichtung der Gesell-
schaft und sei Geschichten aus dem Wege gegangen, wenn sie
ihm befangen schienen in nur einem Menschen, oder zweien,
müßig, unverantwortlich, unstatthaft. Und doch, so die
Antithese, vollziehe das menschliche Leben sich am ein-
zelnen Ich, oder verfehle sich daran. Nirgends sonst."[18]

De Catt duplicates in his own life the life of his author, which begins, however, by way of transposing autobiography into fiction, in the nineteen thirties, that is, the decade before Johnson's own.   Through this device Johnson as de Catt can confront the great German catastrophe, the Nazi era and its persecution of the Jews, the final stages of which he experienced but in an indirect fashion and without being aware of his personal involvement.   De Catt, who is a foundling, gives himself another name: Joe Hinterhand. The protagonist of **Skizze eines Verunglückten** (there is a first-person narrator) explains that "Hinterhand" designates the last player to start participating in a card game. Thus he portrays himself symbolically as someone who never takes part in social situations precipitously; he interacts, if at all, with reserve and caution, and only under the condition that his own standards will remain intact. Another implication of the name Hinterhand concerns the suggestion of duplicity, something that occurs "hinter der Hand," shielded from public view.   Hinterhand's story subsequently becomes a matter of the coalescence of his private and public worlds, the world of a not undistinguished author (de Catt) who tries to come to terms with a politically corrupt age and a beleaguered individual (Hinterhand) who is betrayed in his struggle to maintain his integrity and sense of purpose.

The flight of the book's protagonist from Nazi Germany,

which he is forced to undertake since he is convinced, because of his unknown origins, that he must be a Jew, symbolizes two of Johnson's contentions, first that the individual is born subject to the forces of circumstance,
that is, history, and secondly that personal integrity cannot be maintained by ignoring the conditions which endanger
it (with his Christian upbringing de Catt might have risked
not being unmasked as a Jew). De Catt's exile first in
England and then in the United States resembles Johnson's
attempt to escape political commitments in East and West
Germany and association with their politics by brief stays
in the United States and a protracted one in England; like
Gesine Johnson keeps searching for a "moral Switzerland."
Although de Catt (or Hinterhand) has succeeded in warding
off sociopolitical attacks against the bastion of his self-
sufficiency by living in less totalitarian countries, he has
taken with him his sense of moral probity, which the author
of the **Skizze eines Verunglückten** has called the soul of
the individual (p. 25). It makes him vulnerable to an
attack from within. At this point in the short novel or
Novelle the events related by de Catt lose a great deal of
their fictitious aspect, and Johnson deals openly with the
disintegration of his marriage. De Catt's wife, whom he
has persuaded to leave Germany for a life in exile with
him and who has become his second self and a partner in
his authorship, is revealed to have been unfaithful to him

over a period of time in the not too distant past. Elisabeth Johnson, too, it appears, had been an adulterous wife; after a failed attempt to deal with the situation without resorting to a separation, Johnson sent his wife and their child away and for the rest of his life had no further communication with them. In terms of the story of **Skizze eines Verunglückten** de Catt strikes his wife a blow which kills her; after a trial which he expects and hopes will end in a death sentence for him, he serves a term in prison and after his release leads a meaningless existence, which represents the execution which he felt was due him. The portrait de Catt paints of himself in this instance is a mirror image of Johnson in Sheerness in the last days of his life, an individual in despair and a writer unable (for a relatively long time) to write.

As the title proposes, **Skizze eines Verunglückten** deals with a shattered existence; the writer who has based his art and his selfhood on the premise that a sense of integrity must sustain them both has found that his struggle to maintain a public and a private uprightness has ended in defeat. His search for a country in which the individual can lead the life of the just has had to be abandoned; the betrayal of ideals which characterizes the contemporary political scene and which can be thwarted if only temporarily by flight exists even more destructively in the private sphere, where it cannot be circumvented. Ironically, the writing of **Skizze eines Verunglückten** put an end to Johnson's case of writer's block, and while he lived in a state of isolation like a man shipwrecked at the end of the world, he was able to finish the fourth and final volume of **Jahrestage.** There the outcome of Gesine's search for an identity which she can offer her daughter as a heritage and for a country in which the individual can live with an unburdened conscience comes to a better if still ambiguous end. Gesine and Marie stand on the borders of their "moral Switzerland," a socialist Czechoslovakia, unaware that their hopefulness may be mistaken.

Conclusions critics of Johnson have reached concerning the purport of Johnson's presentation of the conflict between the individual as a self and the individual as a social being have been widely divergent. Judith Ryan has summarized the substance of **Jahrestage** in this sentence: "Different modes of resistance [to conforming] or of maintaining moral integrity are explored in the various time levels and characters in the book"[19] and has found in the unhappy event of the Russian occupation of Czechoslovakia confirmation of her belief that Johnson is pessimistic in regard to a resolution of Gesine's (and everyone's) dilemma. On the other hand, Heinz Osterle suggests that even another defeat will not deter Gesine from practicing her pursuit of uprightness further: "We have reasons to expect that she will find the 'moral Switzerland' of her dreams in herself, the sense of integrity and the 'principal of hope' which have helped people to continue their search for the good society in spite of all defeats in history."[20] It would be difficult to account for the novel's length and effectiveness if its premise were that Gesine's struggle and journeying must turn out to have been in vain. At least Johnson's probing in **Jahrestage** of the depths of the problematic existence of the people in contemporary society who find themselves to be powerless to halt the intrusion of oppressive political and societal forces on their freedom to be themselves should not be considered a eulogy for individualism, but rather the culmination of a gifted writer's endeavor to encompass the reality of his time in the form of the novel.

123

FOOTNOTES

[1] "It is an experimental work with (a far-reaching) inquiry (into contemporary social and political life) as its main purpose," Heinz D. Osterle, "The Lost Utopia: New Images of America in German Literature," **The German Quarterly**, 54:4 (Nov. 1981), 442.

[2] Johnson may have intended to produce a trilogy; in **Begleitumstände** he mentions precedents set by Wilhelm Raabe and William Faulkner, each of whom produced as a part of his work a series of three interrelated novels.

[3] Uwe Johnson, **Jahrestage** (Frankfurt am Main: Suhrkamp, 1970 ff.), I, 256. Further references to this work will be given in the text.

[4] Johnson, **Begleitumstände**, p. 413. My translation.

[5] Johnson, ibid., p. 448.

[6] Durzak, for example, makes a legitimate, if obvious observation: "Es ist zu bezweifeln, ob diese Synthese in allen Punkten geglückt ist," **Die deutsche Literatur der Gegenwart**, p. 238. See also Siegfried Mandel, **Gruppe 47** (Carbondale & Edwardsville: Southern Illinois University Press, 1973), p. 70: "Johnson's work . . . typifies some of the literature of the sixties in which novelty of technique overshadows storytelling."

[7] Another trenchant example of Johnson's use of an as-

tonishingly inappropriate English occurs as Gesine tells her daughter about the episode of the "Regentonne." "What is a water butt anyway?" Marie asks in English (II, 615). "Water butt" doesn't exist in American English, the version which Marie has learned.

[8]Schwarz has used the designation "Lieblingsgestalt," **Der Erzähler Uwe Johnson**, p. 96.

[9]In **The Uncompleted Past** (Detroit: Wayne State University, 1983), Judith Ryan expresses the viewpoint that Johnson purveys "an essentially pessimistic view of individual action" (p. 160). She contends that because **Jahrestage** ends on the day on which the Russians send their tanks into Czechoslovakia, Gesine's attempt to lend her personal support to a political cause is doomed to fail. The unhappy end of Gesine's mission is not explicit; she has at least reached the point of being able to undertake a mission which represents her moral response to a political situation.

[10]In another reference to the unique relationship between the author and the first-person narrator of the **Jahrestage**, Johnson allows Gesine to explain how her journal can contain descriptions of events to which she was not witness, which Johnson has therefore created for her. Gesine apologizes for her inventiveness: "Mit einem Mal führe ich in Gedanken Gespräche über ein Gespräch bei dem ich

gar nicht dabei war und Wahrheit ist daran nur die Erin-
nerung an seine Intonation wie Jakob sprach" (I, 387).

[11]See Schwarz, **Der Erzähler Uwe Johnson**, p. 9. Dos
Passos is rather casually mentioned in **Jahrestage**, I, 207.

[12]Johnson, **Begleitumstände**, p. 413: "Uebrigens war
hinkünftig aus der Times statt objektiv, subjektiv zu
schneiden, mit Mrs. Cresspahls Augen . . ."

[13]Johnson, ibid., p. 448. See also Heinz Osterle,
"The Lost Utopia: New Images of America in German Literature," p. 440: "The constant juxtapositions of German past
and American present tempt the reader to follow the promp-
tings of the **Gestalt** principle and look for connections
between the different parts even when they are hard to find
and perhaps not really intended by the author."

[14]See Boulby, **Uwe Johnson**, p. 99, whose words are "an
impossibly precocious child."

[15]Paul Konrad Kurz, **On Modern German Literature IV**
(University: University of Alabama Press, 1977), trans.
Mary Frances McCarthy, p. 105.

[16]See also the comments made by Johnson in answer
to questions put by Manfred Durzak in **Gespräche über den
Roman** (Frankfurt am Main: Suhrkamp, 1976), p. 430 f.:
"Eine Geschichte ist aber etwas, was erzählt worden ist,
keine Botschaft . . . Ich kann [dem Leser] nur etwas

zeigen und hoffen, daß er sich daraus etwas macht."

[17]Durzak, **Gespräche über den Roman**, p. 478.

[18]Uwe Johnson, **Skizze eines Verunglückten** (Frankfurt am Main: Suhrkamp, 1982), p. 74 f. Johnson's last years were plagued by illness, alcoholism, writer's block, and haunted by the discovery of his wife's infidelity some time previously. Separated from her and their daughter, he lived in such isolation in Sheerness that subsequent to his death his body was not found for several days.

[19]Judith Ryan, **The Uncompleted Past**, p. 159.

[20]Osterle, "The Lost Utopia," p. 440. Walter Schmitz in **Uwe Johnson** (München: Beck, 1984) concurs with Osterle: "So wird Gesines Engagement wohl den Lauf der Welt nicht ändern, vielleicht aber eine Tradition der Hoffnung stiften" (p. 110). Schmitz finds Johnson's concept of a moral Switzerland to be a literal interpretation of Max Frisch's symbol which lampoons Swiss uprightness.

CHAPTER 6

TRUTH AND FICTION: A SUMMATION

Although the composition of a four-volume novel is an accomplishment in and of itself, Johnson, in writing **Jahrestage** and the body of fiction that preceded it, was without doubt not attempting to execute a journalistic feat in the manner of, for example, James Michener. The magnitude of **Jahrestage** and the diverse experimental forms exhibited in the earlier novels are evidence of the seriousness of his purpose, his respect for fiction as a vehicle for conveying the truth about twentieth century life and the difficult role of the individual in a regimented society.[1] From the beginning of his literary career, he focussed his creative abilities on establishing a structure of words, drawn from the two spheres of perception and imagination, which would depict the realm of reality and/or truth. As Albert Berger has proposed, his goal was "(eine Symbiose der) Wahrheit und Dichtung, Genauigkeit und Erfindung als Mittel, die Wirklichkeit durch Anschauung, Erfahrung und Denken auf der Spur zu bleiben."[2] This combination of reportorial and imaginative writing which is the nucleus of his theory of how the truth may be ascertained is the fundament not only of his literary technique but also of his **Lebensanschauung.** Explaining the dual nature of the concept of reality, Johnson once made these observations to a New York **Times** reporter: "In each man's life

there exists a conscious past--what you think of yourself--
and there is the real past that actually occurred and there
are tensions between the two."[3] Before a scrim of historical
events, representing their sociopolitical components as
accurately as possible, even to the extent of making use
of actual newspaper articles, Johnson moves the characters
(he calls them persons) who crowd his imagination. Johnson claims to be unaware of how closely the figures in
his fiction resemble people with whom he is acquainted:
"Was (meine Gestalten) von tatsächlichen Personen meiner
Bekanntschaft in sich haben, weiß ich nicht."[4] The fact
that his protagonists have a direct relationship to Johnson himself, however, cannot be overlooked; in the pages
of **Jahrestage**, for example, Gesine remarks to Johnson:
"Wer erzählt hier eigentlich, Gesine. Wir beide. Das hörst
du doch, Johnson" (**Jahrestage**, I, 256, printed in italics).
All his alter-egos are individualists, beset with identity
crises. Jakob's dilemma involves his inability to be himself without being used by political forces for their own
purposes; Achim has solved the problem by assuming the
personality the state has created for him. The non-con-
formists Karsch and Gesine are wanderers, searching for a
political climate in which their fragile idealism can take
root.

What these protagonists and the other persons in the
Johnson canon have in common is their powerlessnes; they are

ordinary, unexalted people. Johnson sees them as victims
and martyrs, overwhelmed by political and societal pressures which they seek to resist by maintaining their integrity, their sense of individual worth. "Ich bin überzeugt," Johnson has written in regard to these non-con-
formists, "daß die 'einfachen Leute' das erheblichere Beispiel abgeben für Lebensverhältnisse in unserer Zeit, nicht
allein wegen ihrer Ueberzahl, auch nicht nur weil sie in
der Verteilung des Nationaleinkommens jenseits allen gerechten Verhältnisses benachteiligt sind; insbesondere,
weil sie jede Verschlechterung der Lage unerbittlich ausbaden müssen . . ."[5] These survivors in the midst of de-
pressions and wars, these outsiders who are exiled in their
own countries or in strange lands, have an accord with the
"courageous man" who carries on in Friedrich Dürrenmatt's
plays despite the historical and personal catastrophies
which confound him. Because these individualists persist
in refusing to become a part of the regimentation imposed
on society by the rise of technocracy and fascistic regimes, the record of their "dull, violent"[6] lives comes
to be a cautionary tale, an amalgam of the past and present
but pointing to the future, with a message for all people
in the declining years of the twentieth century, a more
pertinent message than that in Orwell's **1984**. Justifying
his appropriating this biographical material for the purposes of writing fiction, Johnson proposes that the fusion

of factual material and the obscure destinies of his persons provides true insight into events which otherwise
would be an incomprehensible jumble of dates and the names
of the powerful. Literature has as its aim the presentation of the truth, Johnson contends, and "dadurch ist dann
die Literatur eine Macht."[7] The struggle of Gesine's
parents to come to terms with the disastrous course German
history took in their lifetime more tellingly reflects
what took place in those years than might a straightforward
account of Hitler's rise to power alone; Gesine herself
in absorbing the information provided by the New York
Times and affixing to it the account of her adolesence in
Germany achieves both for herself and, more importantly,
for her daughter and, not incidentally, the reader, a better understanding of the forces of history and the part
that each individual plays in contending with them. The
Cresspahls' relationship with Francine, Marie's black
schoolmate, illuminates not only Gesine's and Marie's helplessness in the face of the political oppression of a people
but also the stream of life in an American metropolis
in the nineteen sixties.

In his early work Johnson's particular contribution
to literature which has set itself the goal of rendering a
truthful record of life is his explication of the situation
of the two Germanies. Although he has disclaimed the reputation of being the one German author of significance

who conveys the reality of both East and West Germany, a
reputation which the books **Mutmaβungen über Jakob**, **Das dritte
Buch über Achim**, and **Zwei Ansichten** afforded him, he has
indeed been the only German writer who has succeeded in
not taking sides. There is no denuciation of the East
German "socialists" in these novels; as a matter of fact,
Mutmaβungen über Jakob portrays an official in the state
security foreces not as a villain but as an understandably
committed person. The East German nurse in **Zwei Ansichten**
is a much more worthwhile individual than her West German
lover. In one of the essays in **Berliner Sachen**, Johnson
explains the nature of his disenchantment with the government of the **Deutsche Demokratische Republik**; it is evident
that the regime's disparagment of individualism caused
Johnson to suspect its politics: "Mancher Einzelne, der
sich der neuen Gemeinschaft gerade als Individuum überantworten wollte, hatte nun zu erfahren, daβ er gar nicht
als Einzelner angesehen werde, sondern als Angehöriger
einer Gruppe. Diese Gruppe aber waren die Eltern, Leute
der alten, der aufgegebenen Zeit."[8] Johnson does not
disapprove of the East or West German government per se,
but of the failure of each to fulfill its promise. Even
Jahrestage, which delineates the course of Gesine's disillusionment with East German socialism, reveals Johnson's
abiding attachment to his homeland, now closed to him behind
political barriers--its landscapes, its people, its langu-

age.[9]   East Germany is, indeed, for the most part, the setting in the early novels; consequently, mention of West Germany occurs principally as a matter of contrast.   Johnson's approach to life in the **Bundesrepublik** is largely critical.   B. in **Zwei Ansichten** has rightly been considered a caricature rather than a characterization of the typical West German; he is much too blatantly concerned with the acquisition of worldly goods.   The appendage to **Das dritte Buch über Achim**, "Eine Reise wegwohin," might almost be the direct result of Johnson's misapprehensions about the consequences of the West German government's drastic reaction to the publication of military information in **Der Spiegel**. Kießinger's rise to the chancellorship was of grave concern to Johnson; it was an ominous sign of West Germany's eagerness to obliterate the past.   Although these matters cause Johnson's picture of the **Bundesrepublik** to be overcast with suspicion and doubts, his evaluation of the land west of the dividing line in Germany is negative chiefly in the sense that it points out in which respect the Bonn government and its citizens fail to fulfill their obligation to establish a socialist republic.   At the same time, Johnson does not, as many left-leaning commentators do, overlook the fact that East Germany has been even less productive in the same undertaking.

In combining the history of sociopolitical movements and fiction, Johnson maintains the stance of the critic rather than that of a judge. That role he has assigned to his readers and interpreters. Gesine's air of detachment in recording the problems which beset American society and the American government duplicates Johnson's own un-prejudiced view of the situation. He does not identify himself with Marie's adulation of Robert Kennedy; Anita Krätzer has concluded: "Darüber hinaus verdeutlicht der Autor die Bedeutungslosigkeit der zum Mythos stilisierten Person Robert Kennedys."[10] The novel's references to the war in Vietnam are neither frequent nor extremely critical.[11] (An occasion for dealing with this war in **Jahrestage** is provided by a fictional element in the book: a young married couple of Gesine's acquaintance decide to separate because of their divergent opinions about the fighting in Vietnam; eventually they, but not their opposing views, are recon-ciled.) Critizing the behavior of Hans Magnus Enzensberger, a German poet who returned a scholarship to a Connecticut college because it was receiving funds from a government supporting combat in Vietnam, Johnson, at this point as a character in **Jahrestage**, while himself disapproving of the war, disavows the position of the leftists; he refuses to maintain along with them that the conflict in the Far East is the result of fascistic plotting. In regard to his non-partisanship Johnson was once given the opportunity to explain the relationship between a writer's understanding of political events and his obligation not to foist his

opinions on his readers; in a literary discussion broadcast
over the Italian radio he defended himself against a re-
buke he had received for not having expressly condemned
the building of the Berlin wall:

> Ich meine nicht, daß die Aufgabe der Liter-
> atur wäre, die Geschichte mit Vorwürfen
> zu bedenken. Die Aufgabe der Literatur ist
> vielmehr, eine Geschichte zu erzählen, in
> meinem Fall hieße das, sie nicht auf eine
> Weise zu erzählen, die den Leser in Il-
> lusionen hineinführt, sondern ihm zeigt,
> wie diese Geschichte ist. Wenn das eine
> Aufklärung ist, ist das keine sozial-
> aktivistische, sie fordert von einem Leser
> dieser Erzählung nicht, daß er sich so-
> fort verändert, sondern daß er die Geschi-
> chte aufnimmt, sie überdenkt, und daraus
> seine eigenen Schlüsse zieht. (12)

The characters in Johnson's fiction likewise demonstrate the right of individual to add the moral dimension
to the life which goes on around them, to judge it to be
good or bad, right or wrong, just or unjust, in terms of
their conscience and integrity.[13] Thus, Gesine does not wish
to remain in the United States, although her daughter wants
the country to be her home, and Karsch departs from West Germany and "the good life." The refusal of some of the principal characters in Johnson's books to commit themselves to
supporting a particular government or condemning another
has been criticized on the basis that they become thereby
unclear und unreliable figures. Manfred Durzak has concluded
that Johnson's protagonists have no fixed personalities,

that is, that they are amorphous.[14]   Even more pointed is the
caveat of Thomas and van der Will: "Keine von Johnsons Figuren ist von Situation zu Situation mehr als fragmentarisch
präsent, sodaß bei der Bewertung seines Werkes die Voll-
ständigkeit der Charakterisierung das am wenigsten relevante
Kriterium sein muß."[15]   It is, nevertheless their vascil-
lation, their lack of bias, their unheroic stance (Lisbeth
Cresspahl would be a notable exception) which gives them
substance and makes them purveyors of Johnson's creed of individualism.   The tendency toward disinterestedness which
the nurse in **Zwei Ansichten** exhibits toward the regimentation
practiced in the DDR does not denigrate her but rather as-
sures her survival in a world in which camouflage becomes
the armor-plate which protects selfhood.   Gesine perseveres
in trying to reach her "moral Switzerland" because she does
not participate in the rebellion in East Berlin and in the
anti-Vietnam demonstration in Washington, D.C.   Resistance to
the pressure to conform, even in the interests of protest,
is the main motivating force in the lives of Johnson's
principal characters.

In the final analysis, Johnson relies on his perception
of the moral basis of human nature in evolving his person-
ages; in **Jahrestage** Gesine tells Johnson, her amanuensis:
"Meine Psychologie mache ich mir selber, Genosse Schriftsteller. Du mußt sie schon nehmen, wie du sie kriegst" (IV,
1428).   However, the validity of Johnson's assertion that

the combination of fact and fiction produces the truth or
reality cannot be attested to by such an appeal to the reader
to trust in the good faith and sensibilities of the writer.
The effectiveness of Johnson's work has a direct relationship
to the soundness of his purpose as an author. The role of
fiction in literature, as both writers and literary critics
conceive it to be, has two dimensions: it entertains and
simultaneously fosters knowledge (**Erkenntni**s) or supports
the search for knowledge. In regard to the dual nature of
this creative writing in the epic format, Johnson has emphasized again and again that his primary intent is to tell
a story; unequivocally, he points out to the interviewer
Horst Bienek: "Und was ich will, ist: eine Geschichte
zu erzählen, mehrere Geschichten, die neu sind und interessant wegen ihrer Neuheit, wegen der in ihnen enthaltenen
Erfahrungen und Kenntnisse, und zum anderen, weil das unterhaltsam genug ist."[16] Elaborating on the subtleties of
producing narrative prose, Johnson has described the manner
in which story-telling develops into the fashioning of a
sociopolitical environment for his characters. In **Motives**,
a collection of essays in which German authors comment on
their own works, Johnson delineates the process by which
fiction becomes imbued with fact: "Much of story-telling
in a novel consists in representing the relations of one
person to others, the relevant relationships which have
brought that person to the conditions in which he now finds

himself--the relations he maintains in order to stay alive, to keep his end up, to change . . . Accordingly one might also call the novel a system of correlations, including the relation to social establishments or to the weather, to which each individual has, after all, his own, intrinsic relations. What is intended is, in the end, a discussion with the reader."[17]

Johnson establishes, in thus exhibiting the principles which underlie his pursuit of the truth, that his objective is to satisfy the readers' need both to be entertained and to be enlightened. Under these circumstances, the knowledge--specifically, of the shape of reality--which Johnson's fiction aspires to afford everyone exists only as something immanent in the mind of each reader. In analyzing the unique structure of **Jahrestage**, the book's superimposition of massive factual material and fictional biographies, Durzak has characterized the general tenor of Johnson's work and attested to its significance in the field of contemporary literature: "Die extensive Totalität des faktisch Gegebenen erreicht in der intensiven Totalität des Romans eine neue Qualität, die sich als Erkenntnis der Wirklichkeit begreifen läßt und also hervorgeht aus der Dialektik von Besonderem und Allgemeinem, die ins Zentrum des künstlerischen Gestaltungprozeßes gehört."[18] **Mutmaßungen über Jakob** also requires the reader to reassemble reality with the building blocks of fictitious lives presented in terms of real con-

versations and events. Like the crises of the Hungarian
Revolution and the Suez intervention in Johnson's first
novel, the political stalemate involving East and West Germany
plays a significant part in **Das dritte Buch über Achim**, and
its epilogue "Eine Reise wegwohin" needs to be understood
in the light of West Germany's **Spiegel** affair. The building
of the Berlin wall instigated the creative process which
produced **Zwei Ansichten**. Gesine's dissatisfaction with
the political situation in the **Bundesrepublik,** depicted in
Mutmaßungen über Jakob, and in the United States, evident in
Jahrestage, bears witness to the malaise which exists even
in the democratic countries of the West. In **Literature in
Upheaval** Thomas and Bullivant have attested to the disenchantment with the political process which results when the
individual seeks to participate in the governance practiced
by monolithic agencies; they conclude "that the parliamentary
system no longer provides a satisfactory link between the
individual and the process by which political decisions are
made."[19]

Through the coalescence of this stream of public event
with the flow of the individual's inner life which determines the substance of his novels, Johnson has developed a
form of fiction which might serve as a model, establishing
the pertinence of literature in providing perspective at a
time when the exercise of conscience is being thwarted by
the pressure to conform exerted by the mass media. Thus,

Johnson's work, although its sociopolitical frame of reference has a distinctly German stamp, assumes importance in
the field of world and comparative literature.   The open-
endedness of Johnson's attempt to establish truth through
the use of the medium of fiction, his appeal to his readers
to reach their own conclusions, reflects Johnson's own espousal of the cause of individualism in matters where moral
and political judgments must coincide.[20]   Johnson's grasp
of the situation in modern literature which requires a broad-
ening of the novelist's goals, an extention of the purpose of
entertaining in order to provide areas which will afford
enlightenment as well, and his capabilities in carrying his
experimentation with the novel form to a successful conclusion, make the body of his work--unfortunately, already
complete--internationally significant.

FOOTNOTES

[1] In reference to **Zwei Ansichten**, Johnson explains why each of his books has had a different format: "Wenn Sie diesem Buch Einfachheit zugutehalten, und zwar nicht aus Gründen der Fabel, so verdächtigen Sie die Schwierigkeit der vorigen, als sei die vermeidbar gewesen. Es ging aber, bei den 'Mutmaßigung über Jakob' wie dem 'Dritten Buch über Achim', lediglich darum, für die Erzählung ein Benehmen zu finden, das der Geschichte jeweils genau paßte und geeignet war für die Bewegungen und Schnelligkeiten der Fabel, für die persönlichen und gesellschaftlichen Beziehungen, ihre Lokale, Gefühlsfarben, auch Ereignisse," Johnson, **Begleitumstände**, p. 327 f.

[2] Albert Berger, "Uwe Johnson" in **Deutsche Dichter der Gegenwart**, ed. Benno von Wiese (Berlin: Erich Schmidt, 1973), p. 658 f.

[3] Quoted by Phyllis Meras, "Talk with Uwe Johnson," **New York Times Book Review**, 72:17 (April 23, 1967), 43.

[4] Quoted by Schwarz, **Der Erzähler Uwe Johnson**, p. 96.

[5] Johnson, **Begleitumstände**, p. 329.

[6] See the title of Mamida Bosmajian's article in **Metaphors of Evil** (Iowa City: University of Iowa Press, 1979): "To the Last Syllable of Recorded Time: The Dull, Violent World of Uwe Johnson's 'Jahrestage.'"

[7]Quoted in Durzak, **Gespräche über den Roman**, p. 435.

[8]Johnson, **Berliner Sachen**, p. 54.

[9]The extent to which Johnson's approximation of American English retains a German coloration is appreciable; Durzak has referred in **Gespräche über den Roman**, p. 454, to the fact that "Gesine kann nicht mehr richtig Deutsch. Sie sagt z. B. wenn sie Schlosserwerkstatt meint, mechanical workshop--mechanische Werkstatt." However, the word "mechanical workshop," let alone the concept, does not exist in the English language. In a similar fashion, Anita Krätzer in **Studien zum Amerikabild in der neueren deutschen Literatur** (Bern: Peter Lang, 1982), p. 176, has taken Johnson to task for translating the "American expression" "bloody Jesus" into "blutiger Jesus"; the imprecation "bloody Jesus" would sound foreign to the American ear.

[10]Krätzer, **Studien zum Amerikabild**, p. 175. On the other hand, the author criticizes D. E., whose commitment to the U. S. government is labelled an act of "resignativer Pragmatismus" (p. 185), for surrendering his identity--he is "bis zur Unkenntlichkeit integriert" (p. 186).

[11]See ibid., p. 149, footnote.

[12]Quoted by Johnson in **Begleitumstände**, p. 215.

[13]See Osterle, "The Lost Utopia," p. 442: "In two interviews the author stated his aesthetic purpose of reaching

a greater precision in perception, which he hoped would help the reader to find more clarity in moral outlook."

[14]Durzak, Der deutsche Roman der Gegenwart, p. 220.

[15]Thomas and van der Will, Der deutsche Roman und die Wohlstandsgesellschaft, p. 140.

[16]Quoted in Bienek, Werkstattgespräche mit Schriftstellern, p. 112.

[17]Quoted in Motives, ed. Richard Sales, trans. Egon Larsen, p. 106.

[18]Durzak, Gepräche über den Roman, p. 462.

[19]R. Hinton Thomas and Keith Bullivant, Literature in Upheaval (Manchester: Manchester University Press; New York: Barnes & Noble, 1974), p. 41.

[20]See Kurz, On Modern German Literature IV, trans. Mary Francis McCarthy, p. 108: "Johnson is not a rebel and not a revolutionary. He has his own nonconformism. Contemplative nonconformism."

APPENDIX

TRANSLATIONS OF QUOTED MATERIAL

In order to make this study more readily accessible to those
whose encounter with the works of Uwe Johnson has been
through the versions in English translation, especially those
whose interests lie in the field of comparative literature,
I have translated key passages in German quoting both Johnson and his interpreters into English.

CHAPTER 1

(Page 8: "Was ich will ist . . . unterhaltsam genug ist.")
"What I want is to tell a story, or several stories, which
are new and interesting because of their newness, because of
the information and experiences contained in them, and
otherwise just because this is absorbing enough in itself."

(Page 11: "Es handelt sich . . . sitzengelassen wird.")
"In this case it is a matter of an attempt to explain the
difficulties which confront an intellectual when he associates
himself with power and then because of tactical manoeuvering
is left in the lurch."

CHAPTER 2

(Page 25: "Der Verfasser . . . Art der Wahrheitsfindung ist.")
"The author should admit that he has invented what he presents; he should not conceal (the fact) that the information
(he gives) is faulty and inexact . . . This he can admit by

expressly presenting (to view) his difficult search for the truth, by comparing his interpretation of events with that of his characters and thus making each relative to the other, by omitting that which he cannot know, (and) by not passing off for pure art that which is as yet a kind of finding out the truth."

(Page 35: "Ich habe etwas . . . eigenen Leben davonlaufen.")
"I have started something; maybe I (just) want to see what will become of it. Your father would say: you can't run away from your own life."

(Page 37: "Wer nicht für uns . . .mächtig bewölkten Himmel.")
"Whoever is not for us is against us and (is) unjust in the matter of progress. . . The question will be who is for us and not how do you like this night with the dark(ened) villages between the folds of the earth beneath the mightily beclouded sky."

(Page 38: "Soll einer . . . keiner, der nicht gefragt ist.")
"Should someone miss (knowing) himself for the sake of a cause (purpose)?" . . . "But no one who isn't asked (first)."

(Page 41: "Cresspahl hatte . . . war er bedenklich geworden.")
"Cresspahl hadn't found anything further worth defending in the MATTER OF PROGRESS (for what was that anyway?), but he had become dubious about the (phrase) INTRACTABLY DEVOTED."

(Page 44:   "Denn Cresspahl . . .einander nicht erklärten.")
"Because Cresspahl far away and his mother who had disap-
peared and Gesine's risky visit, all of this didn't help (in
explaining), these were just people and what they did to
suit their own purposes which didn't clear other things up."

(Page 47 f.:   "Jonas Blach wurde . . . ihm die Augen öffnen.")
"Jonas Blach was released from Bautzen Prison in 1964 and
since has been teaching the history of English literature
with a pathological emphasis on Marxian interpretations of
social history . . .   And this is someone who would not care
(at all) to go to West Germany . . .   And therefore no trip
to West Germany or the western part of Europe will (be able)
to open up his eyes."

(Page 52:   "Der Leser kann . . . weiß es selber nicht . . .")
"The reader cannot know how Jakob died, because the storyteller Johnson himself doesn't know . . ."

(Page 52:   "Du könntest zerquetscht . . . da passiert ist.")
"You could be crushed between two cars of a train, or fall
from a train, and nobody would know whatever happened."

CHAPTER 3

(Page 56:   "Die Ereignisse . . . Versuch sie zu beschreiben.")
"The events are not related to similar (actual) events but
to the border: the differences: the distances and the attempt to describe them."

(Page 60: "Sie [die Aufklärung . . .eigenen Schlüsse zieht.")
"[Enlightenment, i.e., the purpose of story-telling] does
not require of a reader that he or she be immediately transformed [cf. Brecht], but that he or she be receptive to the
story, ponder on it, and draw his or her own conclusions
about it."

(Page 63: "Er verkörpert . . . einem Zwischenbereich lebt.")
"He embodies the intellectual who is not capable of identi-
fying himself with official West German politics, who also
lives in a kind of social limbo."

(Page 64: "Westdeutschland ist nicht . . . wir es eher.")
"West Germany is not just, East Germany is not just: perhaps
it is more probable that we shall become so."

(Page 65 f.: "[Johnson] sieht . . . Existenz zu gewinnen.")
"[Johnson] sees people as living under the pressure of historical and local circumstances, under the pressure of pre-
vailing ideologies, compelled to adapt themselves to circumstances or at least to assume the pose of having adapted
themselves in order to establish a foundation for their
social existence."

(Page 66: "Er gelangt zu . . . . verstanden werden könnte.")
"He comes to the realization that the respect that people
have for Achim as an ideal person might not be quite that
which it is assumed to be in official circles; he repre-

sents [rather] the common man 'against the government and against the world,' and that his much-admired solidarity with his team might [also] be understood as the people's solidarity against the regime."

(Page 71 f.: "Gewiß redet Karsch . . .Döblinische Syndrom.")
"Karsch does indeed talk on the telephone to his partners . . . And as a consequence he takes delight in letting the reader observe, as he tells his story, how he came to tell that story and how he goes about telling it. (This is also known as the Döblin syndrome [a reference to the novelist Alfred Döblin].)"

(Page 72: "Dabei handelt es sich . . .Funktion ist wichtig.")
"Here in the case of Karsch and Karin it is a matter neither of characters nor types. Basically (only) their function is important . . ."

(Page 73: "Karsch hat sich . . . recht unpolitisch ist.")
"Therefore, Karsch has turned into a very average, confused, somewhat hesitant person, who in actuality is really unpolitical."

CHAPTER 4

(Page 75 f.: "Hier aber sind es lediglich . . . Gefühlsregungen zu beschreiben.")
"Here it is simply a matter of 'two views.' In the main

only two people, whose places of residence, actions, concepts and decisions are singled out. It is just a more elemental story, even in large measure suitable for the traditional technique of describing emotions."

.

(Page 79: "Denn es war . . . für politisch dumm hielt.") "For their quarrel had concerned itself with the fact that D. considered him to be politically stupid; and she had written in her letter that on the Saturday before the (traffic) blockade she had ridden through West Berlin and had not gotten out, [a neglect] which he took to be politically stupid."

(Page 82: "Sie war damals . . . bewahrt hatten vor Mitleid.") "At that time, without even having begun to notice, she had become susceptible to feelings, while in the past habit and being informed had kept her free of pity."

(Page 83: "She hatte unter . . .das andere Land zu wählen.") "She had lived in this state as if in her own country, at home, trusting in a wide-open future and in the right of being able to choose, [if she would], that other country."

(Page 83: "Mancher Einzelne . . . der aufgegebenen Zeit.") "Many an individual who wanted to indicate his responsibility to the new society precisely as an individual was made to realize that he was not looked upon as an individual, but as a member of a group. This group, however, consisted of

parents [the older generation], people from old and abandoned times."

(Page 86: "nicht diesseits . . . zu Protokoll zu nehmen.")
"(He sat) not on this side, not on the other side of the wall,
but to a certain extent on the wall itself, preoccupied
to a degree with nothing more than calling both sides to
account."

(Page 87: "Ich meine nicht . . . diese Geschichte ist.")
"I do not think that it should be the task of literature
to heap reproaches on history. The task of literature is
rather to tell a story; in my case that would mean not to
tell it in a way which would introduce the reader to il-
lusions, but show him the exact nature of this story."

(Page 87: "Die ostdeutschen . . .sich in der Notwehr.")
"The East German communists, when they built this wall, did
not have the intent of acting immorally, but they were acting
in self-defense."

(Page 89: "Eine Vorliebe für . . .erlaubt ist es obendrein.")
"A preference for parataxis, a disinclination toward hypo-
tatic solutions I admit to, likewise the inclination to keep
firmly established the relationship between subject-pre-
diate-object, and accordingly to place adverbial constructions outside of this field, either before or after it. This
has on occasion the consequence that the verb is 'given

preferential treatment' in two senses [emphasized and placed
in front] . . . Here the intent is to entice you [the cri-
tic] out of your reading habits, and even more than that
it (just) may be done."

(Page 89: "Sie war mit ihm . . .du mir mal alles zeigen.")
"She had been with him for the most part in West Berlin, alone
she could return there in her memory, [seeing herself again]
in her stockinged feet sitting puzzled among open shoeboxes
or again pointing with her finger at the unfamiliar goods
in the overflowing showcases of an outlet store, and still
once more standing in the same June breeze before a newspaper-
stand festooned luxuriously with colorful newspapers and
magazines and reading the raving headlines, [all of this] indeed as if she were standing apart a few steps and observing
herself; however, in the (mere) sense of being there with
him all the externalities of the West faded out and were
blended in with the colors of facades, the shapes of cars,
railroad underpasses on this side of the border, mostly
those in the vicinity of the apartment she had had to give up,
and indeed all of this bathed in a wetly cold, autumnal
light filtered through the weather [**Wetterlicht**]; [similar-
ly] she could also imagine that she was taking B., hearing
his embarrassed footsteps alongside, through the hospital
halls and showing him the nurses' stations; however, he had
never called for her, only just once had he said in a re-

luctant, duty-bound way: You (really) must show me every-
thing sometime."

(Page 91: "Johnsons Stil, der . . . beschrieben werden.")
"Johnson's style which keeps its distance from the language
of propaganda, which the author considers he is able to
unmask and mock, can be described as [couched in] the diction
of ideological sobriety."

(Page 93: "Entsprechend . . .Verschiedenheit der Meinungen.")
"Consequently the title also has the old associations of
the word 'view,' i.e., vue; prospect, 'seen from my point of
view,' and up to an outright difference of opinion."

(Page 93: "Ich bin überzeugt . . . in unserer Zeit.")
"I am convinced that the 'simple' people provide a more cogent
example of the state of life in our times . . ."

CHAPTER 5

(Page 97: "die Wirklichkeit jenes Jahres . . . Tag für Tag.")
"the reality of that year 1967/68 as it happened to appear,
while undergoing the risk of confronting within a decade
chapters (concerning) events of the day or the times which
have become irrelevant, even if with the perception obtained
in this way of all the meaningless and burdensome trash some
in the twentieth century had to contend with day after day."

(Page 113: "Es habe eben . . . wie sie gerade komme.")

"It had belonged to the general plan (just) to take up in
this selection [of items] from the life of Gesine Cresspahl the realities of that year 1967/68 as they might happen
to come along . . ."
(Page 116: "Jeder wird seine . . . eigene Verantwortung.")
"Everyone will have to draw his or her own conclusions, as
[a token of] his own responsibility."

(Page 117:   "So ist denn auch . . . man leben sollte.")
"Therefore, Gesine's conscious mind which filters the material
put on the record is also only central on the surface; more
important is, in being directed toward the evocation of the
past, her consciousness as a preceptor of morality, as the
search for [the ideal of] how one ought to live . . ."

(Page 117:   "Auch er habe sich . . .   Nirgends sonst.")
"He, too, had taken pains to show me individual persons
in their associations with many, in the framework of a
society, and had avoided stories, when they appeared to him
to be restricted to a single person, or [even] two, [thus
becoming] idle, irresponsible, not valid. And yet, by way of
an antithesis, human life, it needs be, fulfills itself in
the individual 'I' or comes to naught. Never otherwise."

(Page 124 f.: "Mit einem Mal führe . . . wie Jakob sprach.")
"All of a sudden I am mentally carrying on conversations
about a conversation at which I wasn't even present and the

truth in the situation is only the memory of the intonation
whenever Jakob spoke."

(Page 125: "Uebrigens war hinkünftig . . .Cresspahls Augen.")
"Moreover, in the future it would be a matter of clipping
subjectively instead of objectively, with Mrs. Cresspahl's
eyes."

CHAPTER 6

(Page 127:   "(eine Symbiose . . . der Spur zu bleiben.")
"(a symbiosis of) truth and literature, preciseness and inventiveness as a way of pursuing the tracks of reality by
means of perception, experience and thought."

(Page 128:   "Was (meine Gestalten) . . . weiß ich nicht.")
"Whatever (my characters) have taken from actual people of
my acquaintance I do not know."

(Page 129:   "Ich bin überzeugt . . . ausbaden müssen . . .")
"I am convinced that 'simple' people provide a more cogent
example of the state of life in our times, not only because
of their superior numbers, and not only because they are
disadvantaged in the distribution of the national income
beyond any kind of just proportioning; but especially because they have to pay the price inexorably for any deterior-
ation of the situation . . ."

(Page 131:   "Mancher Einzelner . . . der aufgegebenen Zeit.")

See page 150 f.

(Page 133: "Darüber hinaus . . . Person Robert Kennedys.")
"Beyond that the author makes clear the meaninglessness of
the public image of Robert Kennedy, stilized to the point
of the mythological."

(Page 134: "Ich meine nicht . . . eigene Schlüsse zieht.")
"I do not think that it should be the task of literature
to heap reproaches on history. The task of literature is
rather to tell a story; in my case that would mean not to
tell it in a way which would introduce the reader to il-
lusions, but show him the exact nature of this story. If
this is (a kind of) enlightenment, then it is not a socially
activist one; it is not required of a reader of this story
that he or she be immediately transformed, but that he or
she be receptive to the story, ponder on it, and draw his
or her own conclusions about it."

(Page 135: "Keine von Johnsons . . . Kriterium sein muß.")
"None of Johnson's characters is more than fragmentarily
present from situation to situation so that in judging his
work the completeness of the characterization must be the
least relevant criterium."

(Page 135: "Meine Psychologie . . . wie du sie kriegst.")
"My psychology I fashion by myself, my friend the author.
You must take it as it comes."

(Page 136:   "Was ich will . . . unterhaltsam genug ist.")
See page 145.

(Page 137:   "Die extensive . . . Gestaltungsprozeβes gehört.")
"The extensive totality of that which is factually established produces a new quality in the intensive totality
of the novel, which can be understood as perception of
reality and therefore proceeds from the dialectic of the
particular and the general, which belongs at the core of
the artistic creative process."

(Page 141:   "Wenn Sie diesem Buch . . . auch Ereignisse.")
"If you think favorably of this book because of its uncom-
plicatedness, and that not on the basis of its plot, you
will be casting doubt on the intricacy of [my] previous
[books], as if it had been unnecessary.   However, it was
in the case of **Mutmaβungen über Jakob** as well as **Das dritte
Buch über Achim** simply a matter of finding a mode for the
narrative which would be precisely suitable for the story
at every time and which was appropriate for the events and
velocity of the narrative, for its personal and social relationships, its settings, coloration [**Gefühlsfarben**], and
scenes."

(Page 142:   "Gesine kann nicht . . . mechanische Werkstatt.")
"Gesine can't speak German properly any more.   For example,
she says 'mechanische Werkstatt'--mechanical workshop when

she means 'Schlosserwerkstatt' [repair shop]."

BIBLIOGRAPHY

I.

BOOKS BY UWE JOHNSON

These editions, except as noted, were published in Frankfurt am Main by the Suhrkamp Verlag.

Begleitumstände. 1980.

Berliner Sachen. 1975.

Das dritte Buch über Achim. 1961.

Jahrestage. 1970 ff.

Karsch, und andere Prosa. 1972.

Mutmaßungen über Jakob. 1969.

Skizze eines Verunglückten. 1982.

Zwei Ansichten. Reinbek bei Hamburg: Rowohlt, 1968. (Includes "Auskünfte und Abreden zu 'Zwei Ansichten' [auf Fragen von Mike S. Schoelman].)

II.

TRANSLATIONS INTO ENGLISH

Johnson, Uwe. **An Absence.** London: J. Cape, 1969.

Anniversaries: from the Life of Gesine Cress-pahl. New York: Harcourt, Brace, Jovano-vich, 1975.

Christmas, 1967. New York: Harcourt, Brace, Jovanovich, 1975.

Speculations about Jakob. New York: Har-court, Brace, Jovanovich, 1963.

Speculations about Jakob. New York: Grove, 1963.

The Third Book about Achim. New York: Har-court, Brace & World, 1967.

The Third Book about Achim. London: J. Cape, 1968.

Two Views. New York: Harcourt, Brace & World, 1966.

Two Views. London: J. Cape, 1967.

III.

SELECTED SECONDARY LITERATURE

Anon. **Der Spiegel**, 39:3, Jan. 14, 1985, p. 129.

Newsweek, March 26, 1984, p. 90.

The German Tribune, Dec. 9, 1984, No. 1159, p. 10.

Barber, Benjamin and Michael J. Gargas McGrath, eds. **The Artist and Political Vison.** New Brunswick & London: Transaction Books, 1982.

Baumgart, Reinhard, ed. **Ueber Uwe Johnson.** Frankfurt am Main: Suhrkamp, 1970.

Bauschinger, Sigrid, Horst Denkler, and Wilfried Malsch, eds. **Amerika und die deutsche Literatur.** Stuttgart: Philipp Reclam jun., 1975.

Berger, Albert. "Uwe Johnson" in **Deutsche Dichter der Gegenwart**, ed. Benno von Wiese. Berlin: Erich Schmidt, 1973.

Bienek, Horst, ed. **Werkstattgespräche mit Schriftstellern.** München: Deutscher Taschenbuch Verlag, 1965, implemented 1967.

Bosmajian, Mamida. "To the Last Syllable of Recorded Time: The Dull, Violent World of Uwe Johnson's 'Jahrestage'". in **Metaphors of Evil.** Iowa City: University of Iowa Press, 1979.

Botheroyd, Paul F. Ich und Er: First and Third Person Self-Reference and Problems of Identity in Three Contemporary German-Language Novels. The Hague: Mouton, 1974.

Boulby, Mark. Uwe Johnson. New York: Ungar, 1974.

Deschner, Karlheinz. Talente, Dichter, Dilettanten. Wiesbaden: Franz Steiner, 1964.

Detweiler, Robert. "Speculations about Jakob: The Truth of Ambiguity," Monatshefte, 58:1 (1966), 25-32.

Diller, Edward. "Uwe Johnson's Karsch: Language as a Reflection of the Two Germanies," Monatshefte, 60:1 (Spring, 1968), 35-39.

Durzak, Manfred. Der deutsche Roman der Gegenwart. Stuttgart: Kohlhammer, 1971.
Die deutsche Literatur der Gegenwart. Stuttgart: Reklam, 1971.
Gespräche über den Roman. Frankfurt am Main: Suhrkamp, 1976.

Enzensberger, Hans Magnus. Critical Essays, ed. Reinhold Grimm and Bruce Armstrong, trans. Michael Roloff. New York: Continuum, 1982.

Fahlke, Eberhard. Die Wirklichkeit der Mutmaßungen. Frankfurt am Main: Peter Lang, 1982.

Fickert, Kurt J.   "Ambiguity in Style: A Study of Uwe John-
son's 'Osterwasser,'" **The International
Fiction Review**, 9:1 (Winter 1982), 17-21.
"Biblical Symbolism in **Mutmaβungen über
Jakob**," The German Quarterly, 54:1 (Jan.
1981), 59-62.
"Symbol Complexes in **Mutmaβungen über
Jakob**," **The Germanic Review**, 61:3 (Summer
1986), 105-109.
"The Theme of a Separate Peace in Uwe
Johnson's **Zwei Ansichten**," **The Internation-
al Fiction Review**, 10:2 (Summer 1983),
104-07.

Flower, J. E., J. A. Morris, C. E. Williams, eds.   **Writers
and Politics in Modern Britain, France, and Germany**.   New
York and London: Holmes & Meyer, 1977.

Friedrichsmeyer, Erhard.   "Quest by Supposition: Johnson's
Mutmaβungen," **The Germanic Review**, 42:3 (1968), 215-226.

Gimpel, Jean. **The Cult of Art**. New York: Stein & Day, 1969.

Glicksberg, Charles I. **The Literature of Commitment**. Lewisburg: Bucknell University Press, 1976.

Hatfield, Henry. **Crisis and Continuity in Modern German Fiction**. Ithaca and London: Cornell University Press, 1969.

Hook, Andrew, ed. **Dos Passos: A Collection of Critical Essays**. Englewood Cliffs, N. J.: Prentice-Hall, 1974.

Hye, Roberta T. **Uwe Johnsons Jahrestage: Die Gegenwart als variierende Wiederholung der Vergangenheit**. Bern: Peter Lang, 1978.

Jens, Tilman. **Unterwegs an den Ort, wo die Toten sind**. München: Piper, 1984.

Kenney, Arthur F. **Faulkner's Narrative Poetics**. Amherst: University of Massachusetts, 1978.

Krätzer, Anita. **Studien zum Amerikabild in der neueren deutschen Literatur**. Bern: Peter Lang, 1982.

Lenz, Siegfried. **Elfenbeinturm und Barrikade**. München: DTV, 1986.

Mandel, Siegfried. **Group 47**. Carbondale & Edwardsville: Southern Illinois University Press, 1973.

Mayer, Hans. **Outsiders: A Study in Life and Letters**, trans. Denis M. Sweet. Cambridge, Mass.: The MIT Press, 1982.

Mayer, Hans. Zur deutschen Literatur der Zeit. Reinbek
bei Hamburg: Rowohlt, 1967.

Meras, Phyllis. "Talk with Uwe Johnson," New York Times
Book Review, 72:17 (April 23, 1967), 42.

Migner, Karl. Uwe Johnson: Das dritte Buch über Achim.
             München: C. Oldenbourg, 1966.
             "Uwe Johnson" in Deutsche Literatur seit
             1945, ed. Dietrich Weber. Stuttgart: Al-
             fred Kröner, 1970.

Miller, Leslie L. "Uwe Johnson's 'Jahrestage': The Choice
of Alternatives," Seminar, 10:1 (February 1974), 50-70.

Neumann, Bernd. Utopie und Mimesis. Kronberg: Athenäum, 1978.

Orwell, George. Such, Such Were the Joys. New York: Harcourt, Brace, 1953.

Osterle, Heinz D. "The Lost Utopia: New Images of America
in German Literature," The German Quarterly, 54:4 (November
1981), 427-46.

Pongs, Hermann. Dichtung im gespaltenen Deutschland. Stuttgart: Union Verlag, 1966.

Popp, Hansjürgen. Einführung in Uwe Johnsons Roman Mutmaßungen über Jakob. Stuttgart: Ernst Klett, 1967.

Reich-Ranicki, Marcel. Deutsche Literatur in West und Ost. Reinbek bei Hamburg: Rowohlt, 1970.

Riedel, Nicolai. Uwe Johnson Bibliographie: 1959-81. Bonn: Bouvier, 1981.

Ryan, Judith. The Uncompleted Past. Detroit: Wayne State University Press, 1983.

Salis, Richard, ed. Motives, trans. Egon Larsen. London: Oswald Wolff, 1975.

Schmitz, Walter. Uwe Johnson. München: Beck, 1984.

Schwarz, Wilhelm Johannes. Der Erzähler Uwe Johnson. Bern, München: Francke, 1970.

Stern, J. P. "The Dear Purchase," The German Quarterly, 51:3 (May 1968), 317-40.

Thomas R. Hinton and Keith Bullivant. Literature in Upheaval. Manchester: Manchester University Press; New York: Barnes & Noble, 1974. and Wilfred van der Will. Der deutsche Roman und die Wohlstandsgesellschaft. Stuttgart: Kohlhammer, 1969.

van D'elden, Karl H.   West German Poets on Society and
Politics.   Detroit: Wayne State University Press, 1979.

Weber, Dietrich, ed.   Deutsche Literatur seit 1945.   Stuttgart: Alfred Kröner, 1970.

INDEX